Alcoholism/Drug Addiction:
A
DISEASE OR NOT!

Alcoholism/Drug Addiction:

A

DISEASE OR NOT!

✦

What Causes Alcoholism and Drug Addiction.

Dr. Wax David Flowers, L.C.S.W, Ph.D.

iUniverse, Inc.

New York   Bloomington

Alcoholism/Drug Addiction: A DISEASE OR NOT!, What causes alcoholism and Drug Addiction.
What Causes Alcoholism and Drug Addiction.

iUniverse books may be ordered through booksellers or by contacting:

iUniverse
1663 Liberty Drive
Bloomington, IN 47403
www.iuniverse.com
1-800-Authors (1-800-288-4677)

Because of the dynamic nature of the Internet, any Web addresses or links contained in this book may have changed since publication and may no longer be valid.

ISBN: 978-1-4401-8744-5 (sc)
ISBN: 978-1-4401-8745-2 (ebk)

Printed in the United States of America

iUniverse rev. date: 4/19/2010

About The Author

Dr. Wax D. Flowers received a B.S. degree from Howard University in Pre-Medicine. Dr. Flowers received his MSW from Clark Atlanta University in Atlanta, Ga. He received his Ph.D. in Counseling Psychology from Clark Atlanta University in Atlanta, Ga. Dr. Flowers is a Licensed Clinical Social Worker, in the State of Georgia. Dr. Flowers is an Adjunct Professor for several Universities. He has been an avid member of the American Psychological Association since 1996. Dr. Flowers has done extensive research on Alcoholism, its causes and recidivism rates. Dr. Flowers presented a research paper in New Castle Upon Thyme, England on how to prevent relapse and recidivism. Dr. Mark Schukit a renowned Researcher and authority on Alcoholism was also one of the presenters at the conference. Dr. Flowers is recognized in the field of addiction and abnormal behaviors. Dr. Flowers has been the Clinical Director of several Treatment Programs in the Atlanta Area. Dr. Flowers explores in this book the causes of alcoholism and answers the question of whether "ALCOHOLISM: IS IT A DISEASE OR NOT"?

In this book we will cover:

- [What is alcohol abuse?](#)
- [Causes of alcohol abuse](#)
- [Signs & symptoms of alcoholism](#)
- [Effects of alcohol abuse](#)
- [When someone you love has a problem with alcohol](#)
- [Starting down the road to recovery](#)

What is alcohol abuse?

Table of Contents

Dedication

This book is dedicated to my first wife, Ms. B.J. Flowers who inspired me to be the best and reach my full potential. This book is dedicated to my 5 children, Ayana Flowers, Malika Flowers, Shadia Flowers, Karah Flowers and Wax David Flowers,111. I would like to thank God for a second chance at life. I would like to thank Dr. Leon Kappelman for all that he has done to fullfil my life. I could write another book on how much this one man has meant to me and how influential he has been in my life. Last but not least, I, must with love and appreciation, thank my present wife Karen Sue Flowers for being there and giving me two wonderful children, Wax David Flowers 111, and Karah Flowers.

Forward

This information is about the author. I, Wax David Flowers, was reared in a family of 8. My father was a full blown alcoholic. He drank constantly. He worked everyday, would come home at night and get drunk. He would then get up the next day and go to work.

I remember my father and uncle proceeded to get me drunk at age 4. I began drinking regularly at age 12. I, along with my friends, would get someone to go in the liquor store and buy cheap wine and cheep beer for us to get drunk. This was done every weekend since the age of 12.

After growing up in an environment where it was accepted to drink, I learned to drink and drink profusely. I began to associate courage, wisdom, masculinity, bravery, and life in general around alcohol. Because of abundant drinking in high school, I barely passed. I then went to Lincoln Preparatory School and made all A's and one B. What was the difference? I had learned to not drink during the week and only on the weekend.

I applied to Wilberforce University and was accepted. I made all A's and 2 B's. I transferred from Wilberforce because the nearest liquor store was 10 miles away. I transferred to Howard University in Washington, D.C. because I had taken a field trip there while in High school. I remembered that there were liquor stores on almost every corner in Washington, D.C. Therefore, Howard University was where I wanted to go to school.

12. There were 12 disciples and there are twelve months in the year. There are also twelve steps and twelve traditions in Alcoholic's Anonymous. In Waikiki, Honolulu, Hawaii there is a meeting on the beaches there. In this particular meeting there are twelve palm trees that were naturally there before the meeting ever started. These 12 palm trees are in a circle and that is where the meeting is held. There are also 12 chapters in this book. Yes, there is something spiritual about the number 12.

The disease model (1968) summarized the concept of alcoholism as a disease in the following way. "Alcoholism is a disease which manifests itself chiefly by the uncontrollable drinking of the victim, who is known as an alcoholic. It is a progressive disease, which, left untreated, grows more virulent year by year, driving its victims further and further from the normal world and deeper and deeper into an abyss which has only two outlets: insanity or death." The disease model provides a specific, straightforward goal for treatment -- total abstinence. Its assumption underlies many of the treatment programs for alcoholism, including Alcoholic's Anonymous.

Introduction

Alcoholism and addiction are used interchangeably in this book. The two words are synonymous. Alcoholism has been present since almost the beginning of time. Alcoholism has also been a mystery for as long as it has been around. Surveys since the 1960's have consistently found that about 1 in 10 American adults in the general population has significant problems related to his or her own use of alcohol. Substance use disorders, in fact, are the most frequently occurring comorbid disorders among those with mental health problems. Add to this the fact that problem drinking and drug use also adversely affect the lives of others. Alcohol and other drug problems represent one of the most serious threats to clients' lives and health. Alcohol is involved in nearly half of traffic fatalities and a substantial proportion of violent deaths, suicides, drowning, falls, and other fatal accidents, constituting (after Aids) the leading contributor to death among young people. Alcohol abuse alone is involved in at least 100,000 premature deaths per year and contributes a significant share to health care costs. Why is it that some individuals are able to drink alcohol and have no problem stopping? Yet, there are countless others who are unable to stop drinking on their own. Why is it that some individuals chose to throw away illustrious careers and sleep out in the elements just to drink alcohol? This group seems to be possessed by a demon that commands them to drink. As Senator Edmund Muskie, would ask his daughter who was afflicted by this terrible thing ""Alcoholism" "Who is ahead today, you or the demons?" The meaning is, "Are you drinking today or not?" It should be pointed out that his daughter came from a very wealthy and prominent family. Senator Edmund Muskie ran for U.S. president in 1968. His daughter was found dead in the snow. She was on her way home. She passed out in the snow from drinking too much. She was once sober for nine years. She relapsed, started drinking again and was unable to stop. An amazing property of this illness is that once a person stops drinking for over a year and relapses; it is very difficult to stop drinking again. They will come back to AA and get 3 months, 6 months, sometimes even 3 to 4 years. A case in point is a well known person in the 12-step program in Atlanta, had 12 years of sobriety. This person began drinking beer, thinking that since they were really addicted to Heroin. He thought that a beer won't hurt me because I really don't like beer and besides that Heroin is really my problem. He thought to himself that, "I will never do heroin again. Within 6 months of drinking the beer, he was found dead in his mother's bathroom with a needle in his arm. His brother stated that before he died, he stayed drunk 24 hours a day.

His brother stated that this person had to be physically put into the bed every night. This person couldn't stop using once he started back. This person had over 10 years of clinical experience in the field of addiction. He was very knowledgeable. He gave workshops. However, armed with all of this knowledge, he could not stop using once he started back. He was 10 years worse off when he started back. This is a testament that alcoholism is a physically progressive illness.

During the last months of her life, Caroline Muskie, was drinking around the clock. She was so intoxicated that even though she was lying face down in the snow, she never woke up and was found dead the next day. Now this is not a condemnation of Caroline Muskie, but a testament to how powerful alcoholism is. An amazing property of this illness is that once a person stops drinking for over a year and relapses; it is very difficult to stop drinking again. These people that relapse after a year, seldom ever get sober again.   The question that this book will address is whether or not Alcoholism is a disease or a moral weakness.

As the alcoholism progresses, the alcoholic comes to center his or her life around the use of alcohol. Alcohol is the axis around which the **alcoholic's life revolves.   Alcohol** comes to assume a role of "central importance" for both the alcoholic and the alcoholic's family.

It is difficult for those who have never been addicted to chemicals to understand the importance that the addict attaches to the chemical. The addicted person will demonstrate a preoccupation with his or her chemical use, and will protect his or her source of chemicals. To illustrate this point, it is not uncommon for alcoholics to admit that, if it came down to a choice, they would choose alcohol over friends, lovers, family or even a job. By the way the job is usually the last to go. The reason is that the job is a source of income that provides for the alcohol.

This reality is hard for the non-addict to understand. The grim truth is that the active addict is, in a sense, insane. Other people, other commitments, take on a role of secondary importance. Alcoholics "never seem to out-grow the self-centeredness of the child" The alcoholic demonstrates an ongoing preoccupation with the chemical use. There is an exaggerated concern about maintaining one's supply of the drug. As the disease of addiction progresses, the individual comes to center his or her life around continued use of the chemical. This is a reflection of the obsession with alcohol. To support his or her addiction, the individual must renounce more and more of his or her self in favor of new beliefs and behaviors that make continued drug use possible. The alcoholic's brain becomes literally hijacked to the point that all the person thinks about is getting his or her drug of choice. This is the spiritual illness that is found in addiction, for the individual comes to believe that "nothing should come between me and my drug use!" No price is too high, nor is any behavior unthinkable if it allows further drug use. There have been cases where surgeons addicted to fentanel, a highly addictive narcotic, have actually shot up in the operating room of the very same patient that they were treating. Nor is it uncommon for very beautiful women to prostitute themselves for alcohol or drugs. As the economic, persona, and social cost of continued drug use mount, the individual will lie, cheat, and steal to maintain his or her addiction. The addicted persons have been known to sell prized possessions, steal money from trust accounts, misdirect medications prescribed for patients, deny any significant feelings for a spouse or family members, and engage in theft-all in order to maintain the addiction. Most Americans consider alcoholism or drug addiction a moral or ethical issue, a psychological problem, a lack of discipline, or at best some sort of psychiatric disorder.

Substance abuse cannot be dealt with adequately until it is recognized as a primary disease. The disease stands on its own.

The key to the mystery of why addicts continue to abuse alcohol or drugs lies in this word: disease. One of five abusers continues to abuse because they have a disease, independent of the type of mood-altering drug that is individual and unique. Substance abuse is a multi-factorial disease in that singly, the medical model, the psychiatric model, the social worker model, or the clergy model is not going to work. Together they will work.

The disease of substance abuse is characterized by a primary symptom of compulsivity-the compulsive, illogical, irresponsible act of going back to the drug. It is important for us to understand compulsivity because everyday there are phone calls from spouses and significant others expressing the "if" and the "why": "If he loved me more he would not continue to drink". If she were a better mother or a better wife, she would not continue to take the Valium". "If he really cared about the job, he would not be taking grass or booze." If he really loved his wife and children he would not be spending all of his money on crack cocaine". "He makes $2 million dollars a year as our best pitcher: why does he continue to use cocaine?" The recurring question is. Why do they continue?

The answer is simply this: addiction is a disease, not a weakness or symptom of something else, and the number one symptom is compulsivity-the continuation of the drug despite experience, logic, insight, reason and advice.

With most diseases there is physical evidence of the disease. For example if a person had cancer we can see the cancerous cells under a microscope or if a person had AIDS we can see the weight loss, the deterioration in the body and the like. If a person had cirrhosis of the liver there is evidence of this because the liver swells and blows up like a   balloon. But with alcoholism there is no physical evidence of a disease. A person with alcoholism looks just like any other "normal" person. So therefore, is Alcoholism a disease or is it a lack of willpower. That my friend is what this book is going to address. Alcoholism: is it a disease or not.

During the last several years, more and more research has been done on alcoholism in this society. According to statistics there are over ten million alcoholics in this country.

According to World Health Surveys, Inc., there were approximately 100,000 deaths in 2007 attributed directly to alcohol and drugs. Of these, 18,500 were directly related to cirrhosis of the liver or to alcohol dependency syndrome; 10,600 deaths were related to other diseases caused by alcohol; 9,200 were alcohol caused cancers; 40,000 were accidents-caused deaths by alcohol; 21,000 were alcohol-caused deaths by violence. Various diseases exist at the time of death, e.g. stroke, cancer, pneumonia; these illnesses are frequently listed on death certificates as the cause of death. Yet these illnesses may have taken years to develop, growing slowly, unnoticed under the steady onslaught of acetalaldehyde, of alcohol..

Clearly alcoholism has a wide variety of individual and social effects. The costs of alcohol consumption are well illustrated by a wide variety of statistics. For example, according to an NIAAA study alcohol has been implicated in 67% of all child abuse cases, 40% of all forcible rapes, 51% of felonies, 52% of traffic deaths, 40% of fire fatalities, 50% of all homicides and 33% of all suicides.

In addition, 20-40 % of hospital beds in the U.S. are filled with patients whose illnesses are alcohol-related. Alcoholics are vulnerable to a number of diseases caused directly by alcoholism (e.g. cirrhosis of the liver and various brain diseases) and are more susceptible to a number of other diseases and infections not directly caused by heavy drinking. In fact, along with cancer and heart disease, alcoholics is one of the three leading causes of death by disease in the U.S. on average, the life-span of the alcoholics is shortened by 10 to 12 years.

Alcoholism also contributes to the deterioration of the mental health of family members, and often, to the breakdown of family life. Researchers estimate that the divorce and separation rate is four to twelve time higher in alcoholic 8 families than in comparable, nonalcoholic populations. The social and economic costs of alcoholism are also high. In 1986, it was estimated that $2 billion were spent on health and welfare services on alcoholics and drug addicts in the U.S. In 19, the total economic cost of alcoholism and problem drinking in the U.S. was estimated to be $117 billion. Research has consistently indicated that the stereotype of the alcoholic as a "skid row bum" is an unrealistic one. In fact, it has been estimated that this stereotype only describes 5% of the alcoholics in the U.S. **(NIAAA,2005).** Instead, most alcoholics (95%) are either employed or employable and vary widely in terms of personal, social, and economic characteristics and drinking habits. For example, some alcoholics come from the best educated sectors of society, while others come from the worst, and while some alcoholics drink daily, others drink in "binges". In terms of gender, it is estimated that 7.3% of men and 1.3% of women are alcoholics.

Because various diseases exist at the time of death, e.g., stroke, cancer, pneumonia, these illnesses are frequently listed on death certificates as the cause of death. Yet these illnesses may have taken years to develop, growing slowly, unnoticed under the steady onslaught of acetalaldehyde, of alcohol.

Alcoholism has been grossly ignored and blatantly overlooked as being the number one culprit of the physical and mental health problems of this country.

In general, alcoholism refers to the repetitive ingestion of alcoholic beverages to such a degree that repeated use of the chemical continues to harm the drinker. This harm may be physical, mental, social, or economic. At various times, according to various sources, alcoholism has been viewed as a disease, an addiction, a learned response to crisis, a symptom of an underlying psychological or physical disorder, or a combination of these factors.

Formal definitions of alcoholism depend largely on the point of view of the definer. Professionals, other than those in the mental health field, are interested in developing a consistent definition of alcoholism. For example, epidemiologists define alcoholism in terms that permit the identification of alcoholics in the population i.e., they rely on measures of frequency and quantity and or behavioral features. Legal definitions on the other hand, tend to emphasize drinking that endangers others or the drinker.

In general, behavioral, rather than physiological or pharmacological signs, are more reliable for both defining and diagnosing alcoholism. Most of the definitions of alcoholism of interest to mental health professionals include mention of at least one or more of the following aspects of alcohol use and most include reference to the consequences of alcoholism as well as its symptoms. Consumption of large quantities of alcohol over an extended period of time .Physiological evidence of ethanol addiction (e.g., a withdrawal syndrome following cessation of drinking) Abnormal and chronic loss of control over drinking behaviors (i.e. inability to refrain from drinking and/or to stop drinking once the first drink has been taken) .Persistent damage to health (e.g. cirrhosis) and/or social or economic status (e.g., loss of family, friends, job).

A definition which includes all four aspects of alcohol use is illustrated by one provided by the World Health Organization. This definition states that alcoholics are "those excessive drinkers whose dependence on alcohol has attained such a degree that it shows a noticeable mental disturbance or an interference with their bodily or mental health.

Perhaps the most controversial issue related to defining alcoholism is whether or not it should be considered a physical disease. Implicit in the definition of alcoholism as a disease is the notion that the person experiencing harm from drinking would change his\her behavior if he\she could. The alcoholic's failure to do so would seem to indicate that the alcoholic cannot help himself\herself, that he\she has lost control over drinking. Although several authorities have challenged the disease model of alcoholism, the majority of definitions of alcoholism and alcoholics in the literature reflect the use of at least some aspects of the disease concept. A frequently cited definition which explicitly defines alcoholism as a disease. "Alcoholism is a chronic disease manifested by repeated implicative drinking so as to cause injury to the drinker's health or to his social or economic functioning. This book is primarily interested in whether alcoholism is actually a disease or a defect in ones moral fiber. After all, with most diseases the physical evidence or characteristics of the malady are visibly evident. For example, if someone had cancer, there would be physical evidence of the cancer cells deteriorating and being destroyed. The person would show physical evidence of deterioration. We could look at the cells under a microscope and see the difference between a normal healthy cell and a cancerous cell. The evidence of this deterioration would be visible.

However, a person that has the disease of alcoholism looks like anyone else. The cells of the body are not distinguishable as they would be with a person that had cancer and a person that did not have cancer. There is no way to physically look at some one and on this fact alone say that this person is an alcoholic. So the question arises. Is Alcoholism a disease or is calling alcoholism a disease really a cop out or an excuse for careless, irresponsible behavior. Let's look at it and let the proof be in the pudding.

Alcoholism is a Biogenetic-Psycho-Social-Disease. This book will answer the question of whether or not addiction is a disease from a biological, genetic, psychological, and social standpoint. When these characteristics are all put together then the question can be answered of whether "Addiction Is A Disease Or Not."

I

Biological

✦

First let us look at it from a biological aspect. Studies have shown that what makes the alcoholic different from the non-alcoholic is that the alcoholic has what is known as "the alcoholic liver". The alcoholic's liver is not capable of breaking down alcohol and excreting it. The alcoholic's liver does not possess the enzyme that is capable of breaking down the alcohol. Therefore the alcohol settles in the alcoholic's liver. The alcoholic then becomes addicted to the alcohol. As a result of this phenomenon the liver develops into fatty liver swells and eventually becomes cirrhotic. Most alcoholics die from cirrhosis of the liver. The non-alcoholic does have the necessary enzyme in his liver to breakdown the alcohol. The alcohol is broken down and excreted through the normal elimination process of body functions. The alcohol never settles in the liver and does not therefore cause the liver to harden and become cirrhotic. Therefore this proves that the liver is different in the non-alcoholic and the alcoholic. This is the first way that the non-alcoholic and the alcoholic is different.

The second manner that the alcoholic and the non-alcoholic are different biologically is the amount of electrical energy in the brain. EEG (Electroencephalogram) patterns have implicated this phenomenon. In one study, it was found that young sons of alcoholic fathers have a higher frequency of EEG activity than sons on non-alcoholic fathers. High EEG sequences is inheritable and is often found in adult alcoholics. Because **alcohol is known to slow brain activity, it may be that alcoholics are individuals who learn to reduce genetically determined fast brain wave activity by drinking. Because of this added electrical energy in the brain, the alcoholic's brain is literally on fire or racing. The alcoholic is drinking to put the fire out or to stop his brain from racing. The non-alcoholic does not have this problem.**

The third manner in which the alcoholic is different from the non-alcoholic is that in the alcoholic, the alcohol produces a morphine-like chemical in the brain called THIQ (Tetrahydraisoquinone) . There is an explanation of how this THIQ phenomenon came about. There was female medical student in her residency that observed many vagrants passed out on the ground. She began to ponder the question of why is it that some individuals chose to sleep out in the elements, in the cold rain and on the ground when these same individuals could have a nice comfortable place to live if they would stop drinking.

However, many of these individuals chose to live on skid row and continue drinking. Skid row is a place where it is possible to find a medical doctor, a PhD college professor, a dentist, and the like. These individuals hale from very good families. Yet they chose to live on skid row and drink cheap alcohol. This medical student continued to ponder this question. She postulated that the difference had something to do with the brain of these individuals. She then *began* picking up the cadavers along skid row and taking them back to the laboratory at the medical school. She then cut the skull open of these skid row derelicts to expose the brain. She found that in each of the derelicts brain there was THIQ or the common name is *heroin. She* theorized that this is impossible because these derelicts could not afford heroin because they could barely afford enough money to buy cheap wine let alone heroin. That's why we call them winos. So, the question was asked, "How could these derelicts have heroin in their brains when they could not afford to buy the heroin. THIQ is similar to heroin. In other words when the alcoholic drinks alcohol, the alcohol is converted into THIQ or heroin. Heroin is the second most addictive substance that there is. The most addictive is cocaine. The alcoholic then becomes addicted alcohol and will do anything to get the alcohol just as a heroin addict will do anything to get heroin. This biochemical difference is responsible for alcohol addiction. THIQ is not manufactured in any sizeable amount in the brains of normal social drinkers, nor even in the brains of those who drink heavily. However, it is found in measurable amounts in the brains of alcoholics.

During the second world war THIQ was duplicated synthetically and used as a pain killer. Despite its **effectiveness,** it was rejected when it was found to be more addictive than morphine. THIQ may well be the prime substance responsible for alcohol addiction, immobilizing the will, rendering it impotent. The nonalcoholic does not possess this ability to convert alcohol into THIQ. Therefore the non-alcoholic never becomes addicted to alcohol and is able to stop drinking whereas because of the THIQ phenomenon, the alcoholic cannot stop drinking. One drink is too many and a thousand are not enough. It is found that in New York City, many of the winos or vagrants were once heroin addicts. Because of the cost of heroin, these addicts become alcoholics and never return to heroin. They don't have to return to heroin because when they drink the alcohol it is converted to heroin. They are getting their heroin through the alcohol. This phenomenon doesn't exist in the non-alcoholic.

The fourth manner in which the alcoholic is different from the non-alcoholic biologically is in the brain area.

Historically as mammalian life evolved through the marsupial stage, the anthropoid forms, to the homo erectus *and homo* sapiens stage, the new brain evolved. Vastly complex, capable of receiving, transmitting and transferring stimuli from all of the sensory organs (the sight, the feel, *the taste,* the smell) the new brain transmitted these signals *to* the **primitive** brain for instinctual survival behavior. But the new brain is recent, having evolved in the past recent millenniums. What follows is very important concerning what differentiates the alcoholic from the non-alcoholic. It was the old primitive brain, the hypothalamic instinctual brain that kept the species alive. For it is the old brain that directed survival behavior to *flee or fight, to eat, to* drink, to reproduce, and to know the feelings that were necessary to accompany and implement these actions.

It is now apparent that these two brains, the new brain and the primitive brain are intimately related to the disease of chemical dependency. For the new brain is where the stimulus, the direction and the implementation of abuse takes place. The alcoholic chooses to drink, cognitively, controlled cortically. He or she says *I* want *to* drink. *I* desire a drink. I am attracted to it. I make a decision to drink; this is a new brain decision.

Not so if the individual is unfortunate enough to have crossed the wall. Then the message comes from the primitive instinctual brain; a different portion of the brain is

involved with a different message. "I need a drink. I must have a drink. I will take a drink independent of consequences. I have lost control to stay in the abstinent state. I require a drink" Compulsion, the number one primary symptom of the disease, is now the supreme and over-riding stimulus coming from the hypothalamic instinctual control center, the primitive, old survival brain. In essence, the difference between alcoholic and the non-alcoholic is that the alcoholics *brain* is different from the non-alcoholic. The alcoholic's compulsivity is controlled by the hypothalamus The non-alcoholic's use or non-use of alcohol is not affected by the hypothalamus. The hypothalamus had a very vital and necessary function during the prehistoric times. During these primitive times life was very difficult. Dinosaurs were present. The terrain was rough. There were no streets or highways. It was very difficult to get food, water and shelter. The hypothalamus is the instinctual part of the brain that drives an individual to get what ever is necessary in order to stay alive. This is the part of the brain that says get food, water, shelter in order to stay alive. Now that we no longer live in primitive times and life is relatively simple, it is no longer necessary for the hypothalamus to provide this function; However this driving force that was present in prehistoric times still exist in the alcoholic but doesn't exist in the non-alcoholic. This driving force tells the alcoholic "Get a drink no matter what. Forget about your family. Drink! Forget about your job. Drink! Forget about the consequences. Drink! Drink! Drink! Drink! Drink! No matter what. Drink! This phenomenon doesn't exist in the non-alcoholic. The hypothalamus doesn't function *the same* in the non-alcoholic as it does in the alcoholic. Therefore, compulsivity *never* sets up in the non-alcoholic as it does in the alcoholic.

A fifth major distinction between the alcoholic and the non-alcoholic is that alcoholism is related to a dysfunction in the endocrine system (e.g., hypoglycemia). Another theory proposes that alcoholism is related to inherited metabolic pattern which produce$ nutritional. deficiencies that result in cravings for alcohol.

Milan asserts in "Under the Influence" that the source of alcoholism is acetaldehyde, a chemical produced when the body breaks down alcohol. Some research has found higher levels of this chemical in children of alcoholics when they drink. (Milan and Ketchum).

In exploring the biological roots of addictive behavior, it is postulated that there was a neurochemical foundation to the various compulsions, including chemical addiction. He offered as evidence of such a neurochemical foundation to compulsive behavior the observation that people with the compulsivity of addiction excrete more of the neurotransmitter norenepherine in their urine than did normal subjects.

The acetone levels of alcoholics is higher than the acetone levels of non-alcoholics. Acetone is a chemical that is transparent. It is usually found in chemistry laboratories. It is used to clean the beakers. Acetone is also found on the outside layers of the skin. Studies have been done that show the acetone levels of alcoholics are higher than those of non alcoholics.

Recent studies coming from the NIDA (National Institute of Drug Abuse) indicate that the alcoholic's brain contains more ATP (AdenosinetriPhoshate) than the so-called non-alcoholic's brain. ATP is the chemical that is necessary to *produce electrical impulses. Hence* the more ATP that is present the more electrical energy is taking place. This evidence of finding the vast amounts of ATP only in alcoholic's brains is a major breakthrough because this proves what has long been expected and that is that the alcoholic is drinking to calm all of the electrical activity that is taking place in his or her brain. Vast amounts of ATP have also been found in ADHD, antisocial personality, and conduct disorder patients. Statistics show that individuals that have any one of the above disorders have a higher prevalence of alcoholism.

The alcoholic's brain differs from the non-alcoholic's brain in a very drastic manner. This is illustrated in a study that was done at the NIDA involving a "teddy bear". The picture of a teddy bear was shown to a non-alcoholic and nothing significant happened in the non-alcoholic's brain. The picture of a bottle of liquor was shown to the non-alcoholic and again nothing significantly happened in the brain. This is evidenced by CAT scan pictures. The picture *of the* teddy bear was shown to an alcoholic and nothing significantly different happened in the brain. The picture of a bottle of liquor was shown to the alcoholic and the whole brain took on different dimensions. There was also a light that came on in the brain when the alcoholic saw the alcohol. This did not happen in the nonalcoholic brain. This is very significant. This explains part of the reason why the relapse rate is so high among addicts. An addict is sent away to treatment. Then after treatment, returns to the same environment that has the 72 risk factors present that will trigger this light to come on in the Alcoholic's brain. The NIDA has identified 72 risk factors that are broken down into four categories. These are: <u>Community,</u> <u>Peer</u> <u>Cluster,</u> <u>Family,</u> <u>and</u> <u>Individual.</u> What is significant about these risk factors is that a large percentage of people are exposed to these same risk factors that never ever take drugs and seldom drink. Which again points to the fact that addiction is a disease that affects only certain people in the population? The answer to treatment is at least six months residential treatment away from these risk factors. This information is very significant because this evidence has not been detected before. A light comes on in the Alcoholic's brain to trigger the impulse to drink. Once the impulse is developed the denial sets in which triggers the compulsion. After the compulsion is satisfied the obsession to continue drinking sets up. At this point, all that the alcoholic can think about is getting another drink, and another drink, and another drink, until he or she ends up spending every waking moment either drinking or thinking about getting a drink. That my friend is what alcoholism is. It is a brain deficiency or brain malady that renders the alcoholic virtually helpless in the face of the disease. No, it has absolutely nothing to do with willpower or weakness.

Case in point is, during the Vietnam War, many of our soldiers went to Vietnam. In Vietnam, there was a high prevalence of opium. Where there is opium there is also a high prevalence of heroin. Because of the devastation of the war, many of the soldiers were exposed to death at high rates. One became uncertain of whether or not one was going to live. To cope with this death and destruction many of the soldiers turned to heroin. Many became addicted to high grade heroin. However after returning to the States the soldiers were put through detox. Many of them returned to their jobs and families and never returned to heroin. The reason for this is that the triggers that were causing the use of heroin in Viet Nam were not present here in the U.S.

That light never came on and the soldiers never returned to heroin use. This again proves the fact that when the triggers are present that prompt the drug use; the addict will continue to use. It is very important to remove these environmental triggers if we are going to see successful rates of recoveries. Again, it has nothing to do with will power. It is a brain disease that is so utterly powerful that the addict has no defense.

II

Genetically

✦

The previous chapter illustrated brilliantly how the alcoholic differs from the non-alcoholic or normal drinker biologically. This chapter will look at how one is predisposed from birth to become an alcoholic and another is not. In terms of gender, it's estimated that 7.3% of men and 1.3% of women are alcoholics-this totals 4.2% of the adult population over age 20. In terms of environment, urban and industrialized areas show higher rates of alcoholism

This is a genetic disease. Alcoholics and drug addicts are born, not made. Realizing that this hypothalamic instinctual control center will occur in certain individuals, only when volume dose, duration, or overdose or intoxication is not the primary fact in producing this disease. Why do certain individuals develop this disease? Current evidence indicates that these individuals have a genetic predisposition. His or her XY chromosome abnormality determines whether they

are the one in five that will cross the wall independent of the dosage and duration of drug intake.

A brief synopsis of genetics reveals that individuals have 46 chromosomes. 23 chromosomes are received from the mother and 23 are received from the father which gives us a total of 46. On each of these chromosomes is attached the genes. Another name for gene is allele. The genes are what gives us our traits or characteristics. There is a gene for eye color, skin color, height, hair color, hair texture, foot size , hand size and the like. Well there is also a gene for addiction. It is located at the P7 level of the chromosome. It is usually located on the "Y" chromosome. As we all know X chromosomes give us a female. Y chromosomes give us a male. Hence, there are more male alcoholics an drug addicts than females. According to this data, one is born an alcoholic from birth.

There have been many studies done on the genetics of alcoholism. Given the scientific advances of the past two decades, there can be no doubt about it: alcoholism is a disease that runs in families. We can demonstrate this easily to ourselves if we have access to a large group of recovering alcoholics. When we ask those who had an alcoholic mother, father, or grandparent to raise their hands, what we see is remarkable. Roughly 80 to 90 percent of our audience will raise their hands. While this sort of evidence is impressive, it does not prove that heredity plays a role in alcoholism. What is needed are controlled studies that allow one to rule out the effects. of different environments. Fortunately, such studies have been done and the results are now available.

In the early 1970's Dr. Donald Goodwin and his associates reported on data gathered in Denmark. Dr. Goodwin compared the rates of alcoholism among adults who had been adopted as children. If the biological father was an alcoholic, the adopted son had a threefold increase in the risk of developing the disease. Since these children had been raised not by their biological parents but by adopted parents, the effects of being raised in an alcoholic home could not have caused this increased risk. Moreover, the rates of adult alcoholism were not increased for the adopted-out sons of non-alcoholics. Therefore, possible stress of adoption could not have caused an increase in later alcoholism.

In another study, Dr. Goodwin looked at brothers of these adoptees whose biological parents were alcoholics. These brothers had not been adopted but remained with their biological parents. If being raised in the parental alcoholic environments was a significant factor, then these brothers who were raised in their alcoholic parents' homes would have produced even higher rates of alcoholism in adulthood. Surprisingly, exposure to alcoholism in the primary family had no discernible effect. The rates for adult alcoholism were equally elevated in boys who had alcoholic biological parents but had been raised in adopted 25 out home and boys who had been raised by their own alcoholic parents. In effect, the increased susceptibility to alcoholism in these studies by Dr. Gooodwin and co-workers was due entirely to genetics: environment played no significant role. Of course, one study does not tell the whole story. We cannot dismiss the possible role of differing environments on alcoholism from Goodwin's data alone. Environment may have a role in some types of alcoholism and not in others. Recent studies on Swedish adoptees by Dr. Robert Cloniger and his cow-workers not only confirm Dr. Goodwin's results on genetics, by provide further information on environment acting with genetics. Reporting on recent evidence from an ongoing study called the Stockholm Adoption Study, Dr. Cloniger points out two types of alcoholism. In one of these types, inheritance alone determines susceptibility to the disease of alcoholism. This type of alcoholism may be referred to as "environmentally independent." In the second type, inheritance must be present, but there needs to be environment provocation for the disease to appear. This type of alcoholism is called "environmentally limited." It is usually mild and does not require treatment. In fact, this pattern more closely resembles occasional "problem drinking" than it does alcoholism.

Dr. Cloniger's findings on adopted-out children revealed an even more striking role of genetics than did Dr.Goodwin's. In the Cloninger study, if the biological fathers were alcoholics , the sons had a nine times greater risk of developing alcoholism. For daughters of female alcoholics, the risk was three times greater. As with other genetic studies, this work by Dr. Cloninger focused on children who had not been raised by their biological parents but had been placed in adopted homes very early in their lives. In effect, these children showed the first type of alcoholism, "environmentally independent" alcoholism. Since they did not know their parents and were not raised by them, these male children in adulthood developed the type of alcoholism that was strongly linked to genetics and not at all to environment. Dr. Cloninger estimated inheritability in the 90% range in these men. For the "environmentally limited" type of problem drinking, heredity and environment teamed up to produce a twofold increase in risk for this milder and more common type of susceptibility. (It is interesting to point out that a provocative environment alone, without a genetic history resulted in an even lower susceptibility to alcoholism. But as science often shows, common sense is often wrong.) These studies by Goodwin in Denmark and Cloninger in Sweden agree that genetics plays a major role in the family transmission of alcoholism. As a rule, families do not cause alcoholism and are not to blame for its appearance in a family member. Alcoholism runs in families because of our genes, not because of what we may not do to each other as members of families. It is believed that the gene for addiction is sexed linked. That is to say that the gene attaches to the Y chromosome more than the X chromosome. In alcoholism, in reference to gender the ration is five to one. The ratio of males to females is five to one. That is for every one female there will be five males. For example, I have been to AA meetings all over the U.S. as well meetings in Rome, Italy and Paris, France. I have always found the number of alcoholics in these meetings about five males for every one female. Is that an accident?

Just as any other genetic trait does, the gene for addiction has the ability to skip a generation. For example Alcoholism may be present in the grand parents, skip the parents, and be found present in the children. Case in point there is one family where in a family of three. Neither parent drank at all. But the Grandfather was a full-blown alcoholic. In the family of three, both males became intravenous drug users, the female did not drink at all. She went to a prestigious school and became an attorney. From plain observation anyone can see that alcoholism is much more present in males than females. Go to any treatment facility or detox ward and again there will be the ratio of five males to every one female that is present. This ratio of males to females appears too often for this to be a random coincidence. This phenomenon is due to genetics.

The disease of alcoholism is sex-linked genetically. What do people inherit that keeps them drinking until they have lost everything, ending up in a jail, mental institution or dead. What they inherit is the alcoholic liver, THIQ, High EEG levels in the brain, and the old brain. All of which, lead to the compulsivity or the inability to stop drinking even though there are severe and adverse consequences. This is what makes the alcoholic different from non-alcoholics. Assuming this is a genetic disease, then why don't we see the gene for alcoholism manifested in other cultures. Why does there appear to be a greater incidence of alcoholism in one society rather than in another. Well, let's look at the Saudi Arabians. Why is the incidence of alcohol lower in this society than in the U.S., France, England, Italy, or Russia. The gene for alcoholism is distributed evenly in Saudi Arabia just as it is in these other countries. Saudi Arabia is a Muslim country. It is against the Islamic faith to ingest any alcohol or mind altering substances.

Therefore, a person that is a Muslim could very well have the gene that predisposes them to alcoholism. But, since this is a Muslim country and a non-drinking society, the person with the genetic predisposition spends their whole life practicing Islam and never takes the first drink. Therefore, the disease is never activated. In Saudi Arabia, there are plenty of potential alcoholics walking around, but they don't become alcoholics because they never take the first drink. Remember with alcoholism, it is the first drink that gets you drunk. Where as the U.S., France, England, Italy and Russia. are all drinking societies. That is, it is very acceptable to take a drink in these societies. There is drinking at parties, weddings, football games, baseball games, basketball games, funerals, picnics, and the like. Therefore, anyone with the genetic predisposition for alcoholism in the United States, has the enormous potential to become an alcoholic. Hence the alcoholism and drug addiction rates in the before mentioned societies is alarming. When traveling through Paris or Rome, it is common to see derelicts passed out in the subways in the middle of the day. This is not found in Saudi Arabia because drinking is not allowed in this country. During the Gulf War, the American soldiers had to ship beer to Saudi Arabia because there was non there when the soldiers arrived. Alcoholism is almost nonexistent in Saudi Arabia. because the disease is not activated in someone who has the genetic predisposition for alcoholism. However, there are alcohol and drug treatment centers in Saudi Arabia. Why are they there? Saudi Arabia is a very wealthy country because of the oil. Many of the Saudi's are now going abroad to study and work. When many of these Saudi's become involved in drinking societies, many of them are beginning to drink. Association brings assimilation. The Saudi that had the genetic predisposition for alcoholism becomes alcoholic because the disease become activated. When these students return home from Saudi Arabia, they go into treatment for alcoholism. Thus, the need for alcohol and drug treatment centers Had this person never taken the first drink, they would have never become alcoholic. Another person could go abroad and drink that does not have the genetic predisposition, return to Saudi Arabia and not need treatment They could stop drinking because they did not have the genetic predisposition. This again proves that alcoholism is a genetic-linked disease.

Ackerman suggested that without intervention of the children of alcoholics will themselves become addicted to alcohol in adult life. He noted that there is evidence that alcoholism is a genetically influenced disorder. It was also noted that research has demonstrated a three fold to fourfold increased risk for this disorder in sons and daughters of alcoholics. It has been postulated that there were inherited behavioral traits that predisposed an individual to substance abuse, including alcoholism. Cross cultural adoption studies were strongly suggestive of a genetic component to alcoholism.

The most influential set of results purporting to link both genetic and environmental factors to the etiology of alcohol abuse have been published by and colleagues they have proposed two distinct types of alcoholism. Type 1, or milieu-limited alcoholism, is related to both mild and severe forms of alcohol abuse, requires both a genetic predisposition and an environmental releaser, and is the 31 more common form, prevalent in 76% of the abusers in the Swedish sample. Type 2, or male limited alcoholism, is associated with moderate alcohol abuse (but severe abuse and severe criminality in the fathers), is found exclusively in men and is highly inheritable but not influenced by environmental factors.

In survey after survey, it has been found that alcoholism is linear, genetic, not sporadic or random. It is not by happen stance that one becomes alcoholic. One of the characteristics for determining if something is a disease or not is that most diseases are linear or tend to be found in certain generations and not in others. An example is heart disease and diabetes. Just as heart disease and high blood pressure (Hypertension) are linear. Linear meaning that these traits follow a genetic line. Alcoholism is also linear. Son's of male alcoholics appear to have a greater preponderance for acquiring the malady than daughter's of male alcoholics or sons of female alcoholics.

The fact that alcoholism runs strongly in families has been known for hundreds of years. Until relatively recently, however, most assumed that the twofold to fourfold increased risk for severe alcohol problems among close relatives of alcoholics was a result of the family environment in which people were raised. For example, it was assumed that a child raised in a home in which heavy drinking was the norm might learn that alcohol is a way to deal with problems. According to this theory, later in life such a person might be expected to develop more alcohol-related difficulties than someone raised in a home in which drunkenness was frowned upon and where alcohol was consumed in only moderate amounts or not at all. However, studies conducted in the 1960's began to question this presumption about the all-important role of environmental factors in producing alcoholism. The first type of study to begin to test the relative importance of genetics versus childhood environment focused on twins. Here, researchers took advantage of the fact that nature produces two types of twins. Fraternal twins are born at the same time but share only 50% of their genes, the same as any full brothers and sisters. They come from different eggs and sperm, with two separate fertilized eggs being implanted in the womb at the same time. Identical twins, on the other hand, are born at the same time but actually share 100% of their genes. They come from the same fertilized egg, which splits into two separate individuals.

Both types of sets of twins are raised in the same environment and experience major childhood events at the same age and under the same general life conditions. Therefore, if severe alcohol related life problems were the result of major events that occurred in childhood (i.e., environmental influences), then the twin of an alcoholic should have a very high risk for the disorder himself or herself, other hand, if genetic factors are important, the identical twin of an alcoholic, sharing 100% of the genes, should be at a much higher risk for developing this problem than a fraternal twin. Almost all of the studies in this area carried out over the last twenty years show that the risk for alcoholism is much higher in the identical twin of an alcoholic (perhaps as high as 60%) than in the fraternal twins (with an estimated 30%). These findings support the view that genetic factors play an important role in determining the risk for alcoholism.

The most convincing evidence concerning the importance of genetic factors in alcoholism comes from studies of children of alcoholics who were adopted away close to birth. Here one can evaluate the risk for alcoholism among biological children of alcoholics who were raised by non-alcoholics. It is remarkable that these sons and daughter s still demonstrate their fourfold increased risk for severe alcohol problems, even when they had no knowledge that their biological parent had alcoholism. In fact, even if one of the children's adoptive parents develops alcoholism, this does not raise the alcoholism risk for the adopted child any further than what is predicted by the biological parent's problem. In other words, a high risk for severe alcohol problems is predicted by the disorder in the biological parent, not by problems in the environment in the environment in which the child is raised. The sons of non-alcoholic parents, when raised in an environment where both parents are alcoholic, don't develop alcoholism.

An excellent example of this phenomenon is the recent case of Carrol O'Conner's son Chip. Neither, Carroll O'Connor or his wife seldom drink alcohol. However Carroll O'Connor's son was adopted and his son's biological father was an alcoholic. Even though, Carroll O'Connor and his wife brought Chip up in a nurturing non-alcoholic home, his son Chip still developed a chronic drug addiction to crack cocaine and eventually died from the disease of addiction by committing suicide after hitting bottom. This again proves that addiction is genetically induced, not environmentally induced because there were no evidence of addiction in this person's environment. He inherited the gene for addiction from his father and it was only a matter of time before the addiction manifested itself.

Between 1998 and 2007 a research team studied 227 sons of severely impaired alcoholic fathers and another 227 young men (the control group) would have had no known alcoholic biological relatives (7). We hypothesized that the sons of alcoholics were at higher risk for developing alcoholism later in their lives than the young men who came from nonalcoholic families. Both the sons of alcoholics and controls have already chosen to be drinkers, and this fact groups reacted to alcohol. During what is called an alcohol challenge test, we asked all the young men to consume three to five drinks of alcohol, with the actual amount depending on how much they weighed. We found no differences between the sons of alcoholics and controls regarding how quickly the alcohol found its way into the bloodstream, the peak blood alcohol concentration that was reached, or the rate at which the alcohol disappeared from the blood. However, despite the similarity in drinking history and the levels of alcohol in the blood, the sons of alcoholics showed less intense reactions to the alcohol they were given. This less intense response was observed in their self-reports of how they felt (the sons of alcoholics indicated they felt less "high"), in their levels of impairments in performing a task (with less loss of coordination in the sons of alcoholics), in lower intensities of changes in their brain waves, and in fewer alterations observed in some hormones known to change after alcohol intake. In other words, the alcohol had less of an effect on the sons of alcoholics than it did on the control group, so that the sons of alcoholics were much less impaired than the controls after consuming similar (but relatively low) amounts of alcohol. It is as if about half of the sons of alcoholics could "drink people under the table" from early in their drinking careers. Yet, both the sons of alcoholics and controls reported t us that when they drank much higher levels of alcohol than we gave them, they were quite capable of becoming very intoxicated and impaired. Since the sons of alcoholics were able to function relatively well after three to five drinks, outside the laboratory in a social setting they might be predisposed to consume much higher amounts of alcohol than the control-group subjects. This is because the internal feelings after drinking for some children of alcoholics might not give them sufficient warning at the lower doses that it is time to stop drinking if heavy intoxication is to be avoided. We believe that this reduced sensitivity to lower doses and subsequent alcohol-related difficulties will occur in about half of the children of alcoholics. This ability to consume vast amounts of alcohol without feeling any physical affects is inherited and not environmentally induced.

We believe that the manner in which alcoholics develop the addiction is systematic. We believe that everyone starts out drinking recreationally. That is drinking moderately or on the weekends. During recreational drinking there are no major problems because after all the word recreational means to have fun. Because alcoholism is very subtle and progressive, one begins to move from recreational drinking, which is done primarily on Friday and Saturday nights to the abuse stage. In the abuse stage drinking is done Friday, Saturday, Sunday, Monday and Tuesday. The individual may skip Wednesday and Thursday to prove to himself able to do without alcohol. He drinks when it is absolutely ridiculous to drink. Many refer to this individual at this point as being insane. This person misses the Thanksgiving dinner that everyone else in the family would not dare miss. This person drinks on the job. This person drinks before going on an important   job interview. This person drinks even after promising themselves that they were going to stop because he had already been convicted of a D.U.I. (Driving Under the Influence. The alcoholic eventually crosses the wall from abuse drinking to active alcoholism. Here the phenomenon of craving becomes apparent because the individual finds himself drinking out of control. This individual This person makes a choice to leave a job that they have been on for 25 years with a year away from retirement in order to keep drinking. This person decides to drive away family members in order to keep drinking. This person leaves his family in order to keep drinking. This person drinks before going on job interviews and before going to church. Sigmund Freud referred to this stage of development as the oral stage of development. Freud said that the alcoholic is stuck in the oral stage of development. In other words this person is similar to a baby, this person finds it difficult to be weaned from the bottle. This person drinks constantly. They have crossed the wall. This wall is referred to as the Biogenetic Wall. (The reason that this is referred to as the biogenetic wall is explained in the ongoing chapters.) The person that is non alcoholic will not cross this wall. They will remain in the abuse stage because a red light goes on that tells them when to stop. We believe that this light is pushed farther and farther back in the alcoholic and eventually doesn't come on at all. The alcoholic becomes similar to a run away train with all the lights being green for drinking.

The most important thing about this sequence of events is that once a person crosses the wall from abuse to active addiction, they can never return to casual or recreational drinking. Many of us are familiar with the phrase once an alcoholic always an alcoholic. Once a drug addict always a drug addict. However, it should be pointed out that most people don't believe this and believe that once that they have obviously crossed the wall, that they can once again return to recreational or casual drinking. This is impossible to do. This is what is referred to as the disease concept. The number one reason why so many people are unable to abstain from drinking or drugging is that they try to return to casual drinking or drugging. Many times they will try to substitute or switch from one drug to another in order to continue using. When one attempts to switch from one drug to another or casual drinking or using, this is referred to as a relapse. The relapse rate in this disease is very high. In fact, the relapse rate is higher in this disease than any other and very quickly end **up in active addiction very** quickly. **Once one** crosses the wall, they will always be across the wall in terms of drinking or using until the day that they die. The only true answer is complete abstinence from all mind altering chemicals.

III

Psychological

✦

Let us now recap. We have looked at how alcoholism is a disease from a biological and genetic perspective. Now, let us look further examine this disease from a psychological perspective. When asked about the range of their feelings alcoholics nearly always report the feelings of inadequacy, incompetence, being out of place, loneliness, shyness, feelings of less than, and feelings of impending doom. Now, this is not to say that the general population doesn't experience these same feelings to some degree. But this is to say that one that is predisposed to addiction feels these emotions more acutely or more intensely. We believe that the alcoholic is stimulus augmented. Let's define this feeling of stimulus augmentation. There are basically two types of people. Those that are laid back and seem to take life very, very, easy. Nothing seems to upset these people. They seem to have a nonchalant attitude about life. They some how feel that everything will be okay and work out. This leads to somewhat relative calmness that they seem to possess. Nothing seems to bother this type of person. We all know someone like this. The stimulus augmented person on the other hand is always uptight. This person seems to get upset at the least little thing. If someone doesn't speak to them, then that is a major issue. This person is very uncomfortable almost all of the time. This stimulus augmented person nearly always feels inadequate even though every one else tells this person how good they are at what they do. Example is Elvis Presley. The stimulus augmented person could be in a room full of people and still feel lonely. They could be with their own family and still feel lonely. There is this constant feeling of uneasiness in the air. Some refer to this as impending doom. That is to say that any minute the bottom is going to fall out. There is also this extreme fear of people. That is to say that stimulus augmented people are afraid to face people. Stimulus augmented people can be referred to as the alcoholic. Primarily, because this is the way in which the alcoholic feels before they take a drink. To make it clearer the alcoholic's antenna is tuned way up so that the person that is predisposed to addiction experiences these emotions more intensely.

The only thing that seems to take away this sense of uneasiness and feelings of inadequacy, loneliness, fear of people, impending doom, and incompetence is alcohol or the stimulus augmented person's drug of choice. This feeling of uncomfortably is a signal to drink or use drugs. This stimimulus augmentation acts as a Pavlovian principle. With the Pavlovian principle when the dogs felt hungry and saw food, they salivated. With the alcoholic, when they feel uncomfortable they think about drinking, and often times do. This we believe the reason that people often return to alcohol even though all rhyme and reason say that they shouldn't. Better still we believe that this is the reason that so many alcoholics, drug-addicts, derelicts, if you will, find it so hard to stop at all. Because when they stop these awful demons or bad feelings appear and they find it necessary to drink again to get rid of these feelings. Let's face it. No one,, absolutely no one wants to feel this way or could bear to feel this way for any length of time. That's why we he hear the term once an alcoholic, always an alcoholic because alcohol was the only thing that was found to take these mal-feelings or bad feelings away. Therefore, the person always returned to alcohol. There would be people that would go to prison for long terms and immediately upon release, return to the very thing that sent them to prison, alcohol or their respective drug of choice, whether it be heroin, cocaine, prescription pills or whatever. I might add they told themselves daily, constantly that they were going to go straight when they are released. Many times on the day of release or shortly thereafter, they are all lit up again. Why do they return to their respective drug of choice? That my friend is because the alcohol or drug is the only way that they can find some type of peace of mind in the world. Therefore, the bottle pops out, (although there has been three previous DUI's and threat of loss of family and job,) or the needle pops out, (even though there is all this information out now about AIDS, and intravenous drug use is one of the major ways of becoming HIV+) or the crack pipe pops out (even though the dangers of smoking crack cocaine are exposed everyday on the 6 o'clock news that center around jail and violent crimes.) Why do they do it? They do it because this is the only way that they know to find peace of mind.

We believe that this group of people is psychologically deficient due to this property of stimulus augmentation that they possess and the general population does not have this characteristic. Therefore, the general population can drink and stop because they don't have this need to quiet these negative feelings that the person that is predisposed has. The only other way to get this peace of mind is through the (TWELVE STEPS). What is it about these twelve steps that seems to relieve this stimulus augmentation, that makes it possible for this group of people to find peace of mind and not have to drink again. Why do the twelve steps work and nothing else seems to come close working and enabling these people to become completely drug and alcohol free, when they were destined to a life of jails, mental institutions and death. What is it about these twelve steps that makes it possible for these people to lead happy and productive lives. There is a whole chapter devoted to the Twelve Steps that will help to answer these questions.

Ninety per cent of the population are not stimulus augmented. They are not uncomfortable every waking moment. Therefore, they don't have the necessity to drink or use drugs to relieve this uneasiness. The stimulus augmentation is the psychological property that causes many alcoholics to start drinking and continue drinking. Once the alcoholic starts drinking because of stimulus augmentation, psychological properties develop that allows the alcoholic to continue drinking. Sigmund Freud named these psychological properties Ego Defense Mechanisms. Freud stated that these Ego Defense Mechanisms serve a purpose in most human beings. The purpose is to keep the person sane. These Ego Defense Mechanisms keeps the so called normal human beings from being overly depressed so that they won't commit suicide, or overly anxious so that they don't have anxiety and panic attacks. Well, when it comes to alcoholism, these same Ego Defense Mechanisms allow the alcoholic to go on drinking when all rhyme and reason point to the fact that it is time to stop drinking. These Ego Defense Mechanism are more pronounced in alcoholics than in so-called normal people. During this chapter we will discuss these ego defense mechanisms.

The major characteristic that allows an alcoholic to continue drinking is DENIAL. Denial means "Don't Even Know I Am Lying". Denial sets up in what Sigmund Freud refers to as Defense Mechanisms. The first is:

RATIONALIZATION- Means to try and justify drinking. An example is to say "I worked all day. I deserve to have a drink. or "I pay the bills here. I can drink if I want to." "Every one ought to let their hair down every now and then." Webster defines rationalization as meaning, To devise self-satisfying but incorrect reasons for (one's behavior). The alcoholic has these rationalizations ingrained in his mind that he, as is stated in the book Alcoholics Anonymous, that he cannot detect the true from the false. The alcoholic begins to believe his own lies. Alcohol becomes paramount to all other interest.

The other defense mechanism is MINIMIZATION. The alcoholic minimizes his addiction to himself and to everyone else. An example of minimization is "I don't drink much. I only drink a little on the weekends." When a family member is asked how much this person drinks, they reply "He drinks everyday, 24 hours a day, around the clock. He has four DUI's and is waiting to go to court on another one. Webster defines minimize as meaning to report the lowest amount possible. The alcoholic reports the lowest amount possible without telling how much he really drinks. The alcoholic denies to himself how much he really is drinking because if he admits how much he is really drinking to himself, then he will have to stop. He doesn't want to stop drinking so he continues to minimize to himself how much he is really drinking.

The other defense mechanism is projection. Projection means to blame. The alcoholic blames his surroundings or circumstances for his excessive drinking. For example," If it weren't for the United States allowing so much cocaine in the country, I wouldn't have to be smoking it right now. If weren't for the police, I wouldn't have received that last DUI. If you were married to my wife, you would drink to. If you didn't nag me so much, then I would stay home more and I would not drink so much. It is all your fault. If these damn kids didn't get on my nerves so bad, then I would not go out so much and I would not drink so much. If you had the job that I have, then you would drink, too." The alcoholic is constantly blaming others for his problems. The healing process begins when he begins to look inside and see that he and he alone is responsible for his problems. It should be added that it is extremely important for family members to stop allowing the alcoholic/drug addict to blame them for his using mind altering substances. It should be pointed out that he is using these substances because he wants to and that no one is forcing him to use mind altering chemicals. RATIONALIZATION occurs when an individual interprets his or her behaviors in a way that makes them seem more rational, logical, and/or socially acceptable than they really are. Alcoholics have the innate ability to rationalize the most obvious mistake into it not being a mistake. This is not true in normal people. For example, say if an alcoholic's boss decides to fire him for obvious lack of productivity due primarily to drinking alcohol, the alcoholic can rationalize this situation into, "Good now I can draw unemployment and not have to even report at all." The truth of the matter is that subconsciously the alcoholic wants to drink and the job was getting in the way of his or her drinking. Therefore rather than stopping drinking, the alcoholic rationalizes ways that he or she will be much better off now that they don't have to report to that particular job. Rationalizations are also seen and found in relationships. Relationships that seem to be going to last until eternity come to a screeching halt when the alcoholic reaches the chronic stages of his disease. For example, if the alcoholic has reached the chronic stages alcoholism, and finds himself unable to stop drinking and his wife says that she and the children are going to leave him if he doesn't stop drinking. The alcoholic will rationalize and say "I think that it is time for us to separate because I want to be left alone. I need some space. You and these kids are getting on my nerves". These are all forms of rationalizations. The truth is that the reason that the alcoholic wants to leave his marriage is that he can no longer drink and stay married. Therefore, the marriage has to go. Anything that gets in the way of his drinking will have to go in the latter stages of addiction. The alcoholic tends to make very unwise or foolish decisions so that he can continue drinking. To give another example, this is a true story by the way. An alcoholic was teaching science in a public school system. He found himself unable to go through the entire day without drinking. Therefore, he started to keep alcohol in his desk drawer. He would sip occasionally between classes. One day one of the other teachers smelled the alcohol on his breath and scolded him about this malfraction. The alcoholic immediately began telling himself that he was tired of the teaching profession. Teaching did not pay enough money. No one appreciated teachers, and so forth and so on. The alcoholic quit teaching school and began working at an automobile manufacturing assembly line. The alcoholic rationalized and said that he had made a wise choice because the pay is better. The truth was that he wanted to continue drinking and didn't see how he could do it and continue teaching school. Therefore the profession had to go. Because on this assembly line he could drink without anyone scolding him or at that time threatening to fire him. In fact at that time it was acceptable to go out and get a drink during lunch as long as the job got done. To this alcoholic this seemed like the ideal job until he became so that he could not stay up all night and drink. His disease progressed so that he quit working altogether and drank around the clock, 24 hours a day.

Everyone knows how strong the maternal bond is between a mother and her children. When the choice was presented to these women to either give up drinking and using drugs or give up their children. Many women chose to give up their children. They rationalized this abnormal, insane behavior by saying "The children will be better off. The children will have a better home. They will be with people that make more money and these people will be able to do more things for the children." The truth is that these women wanted to continue to drink and use and did not how they could do this and keep their children. The children were getting in the way. They would leave their children with relatives or total strangers for long periods of time. When it came so that they could no longer do this without getting into trouble, they decided to give the children up all together. Rationalization was the defense mechanism that was used so that the women would not feel guilty about their decision. After getting into recovery, many_ women pursue their children. Many of them are able to get their children back. Alcoholics have the innate ability to rationalize the when other people would find it impossible to do so. Case in point, it has been reported by one that is now recovering from alcoholism , that in the throws of his alcoholism that he went on a job interview reeking of alcohol. In fact in the middle of the interview, he passed out, came to, and then tried to continue with the interview as though nothing had happened. He naturally did not get the job and the manner in which he rationalized his not getting the job was that he told himself that he wore the wrong color suit. That was the reason that he did not get the job. He was able to rationalize so well that he was convinced that drinking had nothing to do with his not getting that job. This phenomenon of rationalization is very powerful when it comes to alcoholism. Rationalization is more pronounced and is used much more and is much more effective in the alcoholic than in other people.

The other defense mechanism that aids the alcoholic in staying in denial is repression. Repression means to bury or to push down. Repression is the most basic of the defense mechanisms. Repression involves an involuntary removal of unacceptable impulses, desires and thoughts from consciousness in order to suppress or divert the development of affect (i.e., to avoid painful feelings). The consequence of repression is the severance of the connection between thought and affect. According to Freud, repression is involved in all neurotic behavior and can affect a variety of processes including memory, perception of the present, and physiological functioning. Repression can be viewed as the goal of all other defense mechanisms. An important task of psychoanalysis is to bring into consciousness that which has been repressed into unconsciousness. Because of this phenomenon called repression alcoholism has been labeled by many as the disease convenient forgetfulness. The alcoholic has the innate ability to conveniently forget the D.U.I., the jail cells, the lost jobs, the pain and hurt that is felt by loved ones. When asked about the D.U.I., the alcoholic will more than likely say what D.U.I. Because of this repression the alcoholic is able to drink many, many, years because the alcoholic does not remember the pain that is associated with drinking. The alcoholic only remembers the so-called good times that were experienced early in the drinking years. Alcoholics often need the help of family members and a very good therapist to help the alcoholic bring back to consciousness the many losses that are associated with a long history of drinking and using. These thoughts are repressed so well that it is often painful to bring them back and talk about them. Primarily because these memories have been conviently put away for so many years. For example, one alcoholic used to brag about the fact that he never broke into anyone's house. Then one day he remembered that he had broke into someone's house. This same alcoholic had committed car theft. This same alcoholic had stolen from and lied to his family. Remembering these things have been very influential in helping alcoholics get sober and break through denial.

The ability to remember the pain that is centered around drinking is almost non-existent in the alcoholic. This is the basic difference between a person that is addicted and a person that is not addicted. That is why going to meetings is so important. The meetings help the alcoholic remember how alcohol has caused nothing but pain. This is primarily the reason that before Alcoholic's Anonymous very few people stayed sober for any length of time. In fact, most alcoholic's ended up in jails mental institutions, and eventually dead as a result of drinking massive amounts of alcohol. There was no help for them. Primarily, due to the defense mechanism of repression, the alcoholic just could not bring it to the forefront of his mind how important it was not to drink. The meetings work because the alcoholic goes to the meeting and hears what happens when someone drinks. He identifies and says "Oh my God, I remember when that happened to me. I don't think that I will drink today".

IV

Sublimation

✦

The next defense mechanism that will be discussed will be sublimation. Sublimation occurs when an unacceptable impulse is displaced or transferred into a socially desirable activity or behavior. According to Freud, sublimation is the basis for all intellectual and creative pursuits as well as social organization and civilization. As a result of becoming alcoholic, the individual that was once afflicted with this devastating illness now suddenly finds himself much better off than he was before he ever drank alcohol at all. This is the only disease that is like this. With most diseases, when a person recovers, the person just goes back to the condition that they were in before they ever had the disease. For example, if a person loses the use of his legs for any extended period of time because of polio. When the person recovers he is not able to run any faster or set any records that he was not able to set before. He is not suddenly able to leap buildings or run the mile race any faster. However, with alcoholism, in recovery the person becomes better off spiritually, mentally, and many times financially. Countless numbers of recovering people have gone back to school and received their doctorate degree, M.D. Degree, Law degree and the like. Many have started their own business and become very successful. In essence, they have more time to devote to constructive endeavors. Many people are able to take this devastating illness and make careers out of helping others to escape the throws and ravages of alcoholism. It is often said by many people who have found recovery that their lives are better in recovery than they were before they started using or drinking. This is the only disease where many people will boast about how much better their lives are since their disease has gone into remission.

Let's look at some other ways that the alcoholic is different, psychologically. The alcoholic appears to be trapped with these feelings of inadequacy, inferiority, impending doom, extreme loneliness, helplessness, and hopelessness. When these type of negative feelings are coupled with DENIAL, then the alcoholic is able to drink with impunity and even drink himself to death. People that are not alcoholic don't have this problem. People that are not alcoholic are not faced with these negative feelings all the time. Therefore people that are not alcoholic are not drinking to escape these feelings. Since they are not trying to medicate these feelings, they can stop drinking when ever they want to.

However, when the alcoholic stops drinking, the boogeymen appear. These boogeymen are feelings of worthlessness, uselessness, emptiness, less than, self pity, loneliness, helplessness, and loneliness. The alcoholic has to continue drinking in order to get rid of these adverse feelings. This is another major difference in the alcoholic and the non-alcoholic. The difference has nothing to do with weakness, or lack of willpower. The difference involves feelings. This is a disease of feelings. The alcoholic is drinking to get rid of feelings. Feelings that the non-alcoholic does not have or feel to the extreme that the alcoholic feels them. Despite great individual financial, cultural, geographical , racial, and gender differences, practically all alcoholics experience remorse, guilt, shame, and self-hatred. Their self-esteem sinks very low and often is shattered entirely. Feelings of loneliness and alienation are common. Depression and feelings of hope

Worthlessness, futility, and a sense of meaninglessness in their lives are typical. These feelings are only augmented by alcohol. The next time we pass a skid row person on the streets, let's not refer to him as a weakling who has no willpower. However, let's refer to him as a person who has feelings and the only way that he knows how to deal with these awful feelings is to drink them away. That my friend is what "Alcoholism" is. It is not characterized by weakness. It is characterized by feelings. Feelings that are representative of old tapes. These tapes say "You are no good. You are worthless. You will never amount to anything. The world would be better off if you weren't in it. You are God's Mistake. The rest of the population got something at birth that you didn't get. You are the odd ball. Life is not fair, and on, and on and on. The fellow we see up under that bridge or passed out in a doorway is drinking to shut down these feelings. That my friend is what alcoholism is.

V

Socially

✦

Next, we will look at how socially, this can be characterized as a disease. Most alcoholics grow up in dysfunctional homes. Alcohol may or may not be present in these homes. However, alcohol is usually present in these homes. Adults are role models for their children. Children learn from their parents. Therefore, if children see their parents drinking regularly, the children begin to learn or surmise that it is normal to drink alcohol. It is not surprising that alcoholics that are reared in these type of homes usually begin drinking at a very early age. However, alcohol does not have to be present in the home for this to be a dysfunctional home.

In a study done by the CEDAR SINAI research department. Temperament was studied in children of substance abuse families. It was found that in SA+ children. These were children whose parents were positive for substance abuse. The SA+ children had higher temperament than children that were not of Substance abusing parents. In a dysfunctional home there are some subtle messages that are given. For example, usually in these type of homes there is little or no hugging. For some strange reason the message is given that you don't hug. Hugging is just not done. Don't ask me why or where this comes from. Usually there are no "I love you's" I love you is very seldom used or said. In these homes there is a subtle message given off that says you are not enough. If you make straight A's and one B, then that's not enough. No matter what you do that is not enough. There is never any praise given in these types of homes. Abraham Mazlow pointed out in his higher archy of needs that we all need nurturing. Nurturing is just as important as the air that we sometimes breathe. Mazlow did a study of Apes in the wild. He found that those Apes that received nurturing survived those that didn't get it died. According to Mazlow's higher Archy of needs one of the major needs is "The Need to Belong". If one grows up in this dysfunctional home where there is no nurturing in terms of hugging, being told that they are loved, praised and accepted, then one begins to look outside for this love and acceptance. This sets the individual up for peer pressure. In order to be accepted, the individual from the dysfunctional home will do almost anything to belong to the group and be accepted by its peers. If the peers are drinking alcohol, then the person begins drinking alcohol. If the peers are smoking marijuana, then the individual will begin smoking marijuana. If the peers are using drugs intravenously, then the individual begins using drugs intravenously. There was a study done to measure peer pressure among substance abusers. There was an instrument used that past all statistical measures of reliability and validity for measuring peer pressure. The instrument was passed out to 50 individuals in a church. The rationale was that there would be few people here that drank and used drugs to excess. The same instrument was passed out at an AA meeting where everyone at the meeting was an admitted alcoholic or drug addict. It was found that the alcoholics and drug addicts are more susceptible to peer pressure than the normal population. This is due to growing up in homes where there detachment or dysfunction. There is a great deal of detachment in these homes also.

Children that grow up in dysfunctional homes tend not to be securely attached. Those children that are not securely attached tend not be happy. Children that grow up in these types of homes do not have a great deal of love in the homes. The latest phenomenon to be studied on this subject is called attachment disorder. Delaney has done extensive work on attachment disorder. It has been found that those individuals that are severely addicted come from homes where there is severe detachment.

A study concerning attachment was done involving monkeys. The study showed that monkeys that were not securely attached and reared in isolation exhibited schizophrenic behaviors of rocking back and forth. They had difficulty forming and establishing peer relationships.

Those individuals that come from very securely attached families tend to have a positive outlook on life. They tend to be less depresses and seem to have a direction and purpose. When, adversity does strike, as it does in all of us, securely attached persons tend to handle the adversity better than those that are not securely attached. Those that are not securely attached usually turn to substances to help them cope with the difficult situation. Substance abuse tends to run very high in those homes where children are not securely attached. The probability for substance abuse and addiction tends to run very high in these types of families. The use of substances by a child whose parents are substance abusers is cyclical in nature. Children who are affected by inadequate parenting and observe the use of substances by their parent(s) to relieve depression or other emotional needs may then begin experimenting with drugs and alcohol as a form of escape or self-medication for depression. Adolescents who live in homes affected by substance abuse may show a high level of depression, anxiety, and anger resulting from suppressed or expressed family conflict or violence among family members. Adolescents in these types of homes will more than likely turn to substances to self-medicate these conditions which in turn leads to addiction. Erickson pointed out in his (8) stages of man that the first stage of development, 0 to 12 months, is characterized by basic trust. In this stage the child learns either to trust or mistrust. In other words if the child has a healthy bond with the caregiver, then the child learns to trust in the universe and believes that the universe is a safe place. However if the child is abused, neglected, or when it cries no one feeds it, then the child begins to not trust in the universe and learns to not trust people as well as learn that the universe is not a safe place. This lack of trust again sets the child up for substance abuse. The attachment between the child and the adult is very important in determining whether or not one becomes severely addicted. Most addicts or alcoholics report not having a good healthy relationship with one of their parents. This lack of strong bond or hatred if you will sets one up for peer pressure. The peer pressure sets them up for addiction.

A study concerning attachment was done involving monkeys. The study showed that monkeys that were not securely attached and reared in isolation exhibited schizophrenic behaviors of rocking back and forth. They had difficulty forming and establishing peer relationships.

Those individuals that come from very securely attached families tend to have a positive outlook on life. They tend to be less depressed and seem to have a direction and purpose in life. When adversity does strike, as it does in all of us, securely attached persons tend to handle the adversity better than those that are not securely attached. Those that are not securely attached usually turn to substances to help them cope with the difficult situation. Attachment provides the child with the emotional fuel he or she needs to explore, discover, and learn. However, in order for healthy attachment to take place there must be consistent nurturing. Surveys indicate that those individuals with substance abuse or addiction problems come from families where there was not adequate attachment and bonding between the child and the caregiver. Parents with substance abuse problems typically do not have excellent parenting skills. As a result, the children grow up not being securely attached. This in turn would leave the child with attachment deficits and in turn, with substance abuse problems.

A study was done by the National Institute of Justice entitled Childhood Victimization and Risk for Alcohol and Drug Arrests. Using data from a large project (sponsored by the National Institute of Justice, Indiana University Biomedical Research Committee, and Harvard University's Talley foundation on child abuse and neglect as predictors of violent criminal behavior, researchers investigated the connection between childhood maltreatment as a significant predictor of adult arrests for alcohol and/or drug-related offenses. The study found that childhood maltreatment is a significant predictor of adult arrests for alcohol and or drug-related offenses. This study is significant because those individuals that are arrested for alcohol and drug problems, typically are addicted to these substances. These individuals sell the substances in order to keep an adequate supply on hand. This study again points to the fact that lack of sufficient bonding by the caregiver of a child tends to lead to substance abuse and other problems that are directly related to substance abuse. Children growing up in these types of homes tend to be very detached, lack attachment and bonding. Children begin to learn to be less attached as a defense mechanism against the amount of abuse and chaos going on around them. These children learn not to trust. When they do trust, the trust is betrayed. Children in these environments associate abuse with love. Therefore they begin subconsciously to look for some one that will abuse them. "After all", they summize,"Mom loved Dad. Dad abused Mom. Dad lied to Mom and he cheated on her. That means that if someone loves me, they are suppose to lie to me, cheat on me and abuse me". This abuse can be physical, emotional, financial, or sexual. Sometimes it can mean all forms of abuse. The individual has the ideal family script in their heads. The ideal family script, is the map that a person uses when they are looking for the ideal person to have a relationship with. Therefore, if you don't abuse and misuse me, then you must not love me. I will go out and find someone that will misuse and abuse me. This again sets up the cycle of addiction. The person begins to drink and do drugs to cope with this abuse.

In relationship to the social aspects of the disease there is another aspect that we should look at. That aspect is Domestic Violence. Severe physical assaults of women occur in 8 percent to 13 percent of all marriages; in two-thirds of these relationships, the assaults reoccur. One-fourth to one-half of domestically abusive men had substance abuse problems. Using the best data available, perpetrator or victim had consumed alcohol in about half of all incidents of domestic violence. Besides the statistical association between alcohol and physical abuse, families where substance abuse occurs and families where woman abuse occurs often share characteristics: intergenerational transmission of the problem, frequent crisis states, and the abuser blaming the partner for his behavior.

Given the high co-incidence of substance use and domestic assault, many probationers assume that substance use is a primary cause of violence toward women. Parishioners are not alone; those closest to violence--batterers, victims, and law enforcement officers--often attribute causation of domestic violence to alcohol or drugs. Most men who use psychoactive substances are not violent toward women, however, and most episodes of violence do not involve alcohol or drug use by batterers or victims. Other factors must account for the observed relationship between substance abuse and domestic assault. Generally assaultive men are diagnosed as chemically dependent more often than not. Alcoholic women receive greater level of physical and verbal abuse than nonalcoholic women. A woman using drugs or alcohol increases the likelihood that she will be battered, increases the likelihood that he male partner will also be drinking when batters her and increases her chances of physical injury. *To recap those individuals that have the disease of addiction are not weak by any means. These individuals are basically set up for addiction. They really do not have a chance. These individuals are biologically predisposed, genetically predisposed, psychologically predisposed, and by growing up in dysfunctional homes they are socially predisposed to addiction. They are like a firecracker just waiting for a match to light the fuse. In the alcoholics case it is the first drink that lights that fuse. The United States is characterized as being a drinking society. It is almost impossible to live in the U.S., be predisposed to alcohol and not become alcoholic, because the first drink is inevitable. Once the first drink is taken, the rest is history. The power of the disease takes over and it is as if there is no thought whatsoever, when it comes to whether one is gong to drink alcohol or not. The term powerlessness is very appropriate here.

All of these factors, the genetic predisposition, the biological predisposition, the psychological predisposition, and the social predisposition are all ingredients that go to make the person alcoholic. When you add all of these together you get instant alcoholism. It is not a matter of choice or willpower. It is predestination. One just doesn't happen to become alcoholic. One is lured into alcoholism. It takes time to become alcoholic.

If a person became diabetic, then we would not blame that person for being diabetic. We would not say that person is a bad or weak person because they cannot ingest sugar into their bodies without going into a coma. We would just say that this person is a diabetic. This person has a disease. However, when it comes to alcoholism we are reluctant to call this a disease. We are hesitant to use the term disease to describe alcoholism. Instead we use the terms such a vagrant, skid row bum, lush, weakling, slave, and the like, to describe what is clearly a disease. In order for something to be a disease, it must fit the criteria of being genetically predisposed.

Webster defines the term disease as meaning an abnormal condition of an organism. Would an alcoholic not fit this definition of one having the disease of alcoholism. Is it not abnormal to drink alcohol even though one has been told that ones liver is becoming cirrhotic. To continue drinking and eventually die of cirrhosis of the liver would be abnormal behavior, wouldn't it. Would it be characterized as abnormal be found drunk on the job. This mind you is a job that is providing livelihood and also providing stability. Yet, a person finds it incredible that they cannot stay sober in order to keep this job. They are indeed powerless.

Another reason for characterizing this as a disease is the mental obsesses ion and the physical compulsion that makes it utterly impossible for an individual to stop drinking on their own. When this individual is not drinking they are thinking about drinking. Drinking is the real motive behind and centered around any decision that is made. The criteria for making any decision is the question, "Is there going to be drink as a result of deciding to do things this way as opposed to doing things that way. "(study guide)

Some individuals are more vulnerable to alcoholism than others. The notion of immunity versus susceptibility is familiar in biology. We are all exposed to the tubercular bacillus daily by have built up sufficient immunity that are relatively safe. On the other hand, it is said that measles, a trivial child's disease to us, killed one-fourth of the total population of Iceland when first spread from a whaling ship, because no previous exposure meant zero immunity. Diabetes runs in families, and although the parallel is not perfect, the similarity to alcoholism is striking in many ways. Humans differ markedly from each other in both anatomy and physiology, contrary to what the textbooks might lead us to suspect: Organs are not located according to the anatomy diagrams; some people are color blind or left-handed; one person's stomach might secrete as much as one thousand times the digestive fluid of another. We know that some people get stimulated by sedatives, and a few get depressed by speed. Why should we assume that all react in the same way to alcohol?

Experiments show that even within the same species, some animals adapt to alcohol at once, some slowly, and some never do. Some mice get high on alcohol, some do not. . Research with humans is much more difficult, because we cannot control all factors and "make" alcoholics, or measure every bit of food and drink since birth. Why do some teens get cirrhosis in eighteen months, and not Winston Churchill in ninety years? Vulnerability and immunity are not black and white boxes, but a continuum with all shades of f gray in between. The research team may require years to identify and isolate just one enzyme out of the fifty or sixty involved, then longer to understand its biochemistry and transfer this knowledge from the laboratory to the living person.

Yes, there are many factors involved, but progress is being made. We now have massive evidence that alcoholics differ physiologically from nonalcoholic, especially in both brain and liver. Many of the differences seem to be present at birth or to continue even after two years of sobriety. Contrary to the notion of a single X factor, we believe that every organ of the body can be affected by alcohol and also enter into the body's handling of alcohol.

Low tolerance did not prove significant in predicting alcohol, partly because early thought here missed the fact that good tolerance is a sign of alcoholism, and what they should have been looking for was a lack of intolerance. The person who is allergic to alcohol, gets the Chinese flush, or otherwise feels uncomfortable or even sick after one drinks, is not likely to drink enough to develop alcoholism. The supposed X factor is not a simple defect but a combination of differences in liver and brain. In other words there are differences in certain individuals liver and brains that make these individuals more susceptible to alcoholism. This is the primary basis for referring to alcoholism as a disease.

Let's play "Devil's Advocate" for a while. Let's assume that addiction is not a disease and that everyone is affected by drugs and alcohol in the same manner. Then we will take a very close look at Vietnam. During the Vietnam Era, many of our young men were sent to a hell whole, that was not only humid it was laden with exploding mines and gigantic mosquitoes. There was heroin there available in the pure form, much more potent as to what is on the streets. In order to cope with these aversive conditions, our young men began using massive amounts of very potent, addictive heroin. However upon their return to the United States, they were surrounded by family, friends, and productive jobs. As a result only a small percentage of our men became addictive to Heroin. This merely means that all of the men were not predisposed to addiction. Those that were predisposed to addiction became addicts. (Only a small percentage became addicts. This points to the vulnerability due to physiological aspects. The fact that 70% of cocaine addicts have at least one parent that was alcoholic points to the fact that addiction is a disease that has predisposal qualities.

Let's take this same premise a step farther. Let's assume that addiction is not a disease and that everyone is susceptible to addiction at the same rate. How do we explain the adoption studies, the studies done by Goodwin on twins. If indeed the postulation is accepted that addiction is not a disease then how do we explain the almost complete homogeneousness that exist in Alcoholics Anonymous. For example, individuals in Scotland, Ireland, Paris, Russia, Barcelona, Alaska, London and in most populated parts of the world attend Alcoholic's Anonymous meetings. While sitting in any of these meetings, most of the time the only distinct differing variable will be the language difference. These people all talk about the same fears, insecurities, inferiorities and self-centeredness. This cannot be a coincidence that these people no matter what the cultural difference, political beliefs or religious beliefs. They all sound so much alike. Even though these people are thousands of miles apart they talk as though they have known each other all of their lives. They have one common denominator and that denominator is addiction. Many times a recovering drug addict or alcoholic will reply that they walked in an Alcoholic's Anonymous meeting in a foreign country and immediately, immediately, felt right at home.

The disease of Alcoholism or Addiction is universal. It affects everyone the same. It doesn't discriminate against anyone. It is an equal opportunity destroyer. One major components of this disease is the loneliness. The alcoholic can be in a room full of people and still feel alone.

Let's return to our former premise. Again the assumption is that alcoholism is not a disease. If alcoholism were not a disease, then aversion therapy would work. Aversion therapy is similar to shock therapy in that every time that a person would drink they would be shocked or made to throw up. After a person was shocked enough times or threw up enough times, they would stop drinking if alcoholism were not a disease. Diversion tactics would work also in that if a person is locked up for many many years for a DUI or drinking related offenses, then the consequences of being incarcerated or having ones freedom taken away would be enough of an incentive to get a person to stop drinking. More times than not these same people that spend large amounts of time in jail, get out of jail and are often drunk the same day. Punishment doesn't seem to work. If punishment worked then we wouldn't need more jails. In fact, there would be less need for jails because those that are in jail now would have learned their lesson and would not be returning to jail. However, rather than needing less jails, there are more jails and prisons being built because the existing ones are either filled or overcrowded. It is fairly obvious that punishment hasn't worked. Since alcoholism and drug addiction are a disease, the person continues to drink and abuse substances until they are treated for the disease. It is similar to punishing a diabetic for getting sick after eating sugar. No matter how much we punish this particular diabetic, they are still going to get sick if they eat sugar. This is primarily because they have a disease. The disease is diabetes. The same is true for a person that has the disease of addiction. Unless, the addict is treated for addiction, the addict will continue to drink and use drugs, and as an added, result continue to get into trouble. Today, there are thousands and even millions of successful cases of recovery from addiction. Many who had lost everything eventually, gained it all back. However, it was not until alcoholism and addiction were looked at scientifically and empirically as a disease, there were few if any recoveries.

VI

What Makes The Twelve Steps Work

✦

What is it about the Twelve Steps that seem so miraculous. They make you take responsibility for yourself. As discussed earlier, the alcoholic or addict has been drinking and abusing drugs for a long, long, long, period. In order to do this for such long periods in so much excess, the alcoholic has developed an elaborate denial system. The alcoholic has been able to blame all of his problems on someone else and as a result has become extremely dependent on people. The alcoholic begins to despise himself when others begin to flee. The others flee to preserve their own sanity. The more the alcoholic depends on others the more he dislikes himself until he winds up hating his guts. He winds up hating to look at himself in the mirror. Self-hatred sets in and he for the first time actually thinks about the possibility of committing suicide. This can be considered a bottom. Well, the twelve steps makes the person take responsibility for themselves. The person begins to look at himself as causing his problems. This is good news because if he caused his problems this means that he can solve his problems. The twelve steps enables the alcoholic-addict to for the first time take a good look at himself and he sees himself as he really is and not what he wished he was. George spoke on this very subject as he delivered a state of the union address. He stated that there comes a point in everyone's life where God introduces you to yourself and you see yourself as you really are. That is precisely what the twelve steps accomplish. The next thing that the twelve steps do is they raise the addicts self-esteem. The addict starts to begin to like himself. The twelve steps help to take the shame away from this shame-based disease. The twelve steps allows one to begin to trust again and to take risk that here to fore these same risk were unthinkable. Using the twelve steps one begins to trust in a power greater than oneself. This power allows one take risk because no matter what happens one knows that this power is going to take care of them.

The third thing that the twelve steps do is that they empower. They give the added the needed power to stay away from the first drink. Staying away from the first drink is the foundation. On this foundation, relationships are built, goals that became a pipedream or something of the impossible are suddenly being accomplished. There is often detected a new sense of confidence. However, it is not cockiness but a quiet sense of assuredness. This empowerment is done internally. It is often said that "It is an inside job." Power has nothing to do with what is on the outside. It all has to do with what is on the inside. Once the recovering person encompasses the twelve steps into their lives, they are reborn. They have a new outlook on life and a new vision. Life doesn't change. What changes is the perception. With this new outlook comes a new sense of hope. For so many years the alcoholic-addict turned to alcohol and drugs to get power. The alcohol and drugs only served to take power away. Now the addict uses the twelve steps to gain this same power. The twelve steps are a roadmap to prosperity. The first three steps are about giving up or surrendering and giving up the old ideas. The second three steps are about waking up. This about coming out of the alcoholic fog and seeing life for the first time basically as everyone else sees it. The alcoholic's mind has become warped and twisted as a result of so many years of drinking. The alcoholic doesn't see the world as the non-alcoholic sees the world. Waking up is about getting in touch with reality. The next three steps are about making up. They are about making amends. This is about cleaning up the mess and clearing away the wreckage of the past. The next three steps are about taking up. That is when all of the twelve steps are taken and applied to life. This makes life much more meaningful and useful. Something spiritual happens. The individual that formally was constantly drunk now has a complete psychic change. The individual talks differently and acts differently. It is as if a new person has entered the alcoholic's body. A spiritual awakening has taken place.

First three steps= giving up

Second three steps= waking up

Third three steps= making up

Last three steps= taking up

There is a new sense of peace along with this power. There is no longer the need to argue or to make points. One learns to surrender to win.

Surrender to win sounds like a paradox. One might even say that this slogan sounds as though it is a contradiction. For example, the question might be posed, "How can one win if he surrenders?" That is the dilemma.

In our society it is taught that the more fighting, the better the chances are at winning. This posture of fighting harder and not willing to give up control leads to addiction, depression, neurosis, and sometimes psychosis. The argument can also be postulated that by surrendering, one actually gets power.

Case in point, during World War 11, the Atom bomb was dropped on the Japanese. The Japanese had never seen or felt anything like the devastation of the Atom Bomb. They gave up and surrendered unconditionally. In essence, as a result, the Japanese own many of the United States' prime real estate sights. One of the United States' biggest fears is that the Japanese will pull their Japanese dollars out of the American banks. If the Japanese did this, it would be disastrous for the American banks. The Japanese surrendered and, as a result, they won. The twelve steps are all about surrendering and giving up the "old ideas". The "old ideas" are what gives the alcoholic the impetus to continue drinking. The "old ideas" say "You are not okay. You are less than. You will never amount to anything. You have to make everyone happy. You have to solve all the problems of the world by Thursday. Everyone else drinks. I can drink, too. The twelve steps enable a person to surrender and to give up these "old ideas". Therefore, their minds are free and they don't have to drink. The major component that makes the twelve steps work is that they are spiritual in nature. Carl Jung postulated long ago, " The alcoholic's problem is spiritual. In fact Bill Wilson wrote Carl Jung and asked him in a famous letter how it is that Carl Jung knew that the alcoholic's problem was lack of spirituality. Carl Jung replied that the alcoholic lacked spirituality and was seeking it through the spirits of alcohol. The alcohol set the individual free. The twelve steps set the alcoholic free. Today, there are over 2 million alcoholics living sober, useful, meaningful and prosperous lives because of the twelve steps. Many sober alcoholics use the twelve steps to start relationships, to start businesses, go back to school, and to have flourishing relationships. It seems as though the twelve steps were tailor made for the alcoholic to get sober by.

The twelve steps give the alcoholic directions on how to live and be happy without the use of chemicals. What the alcoholic/addict lacks most in their lives is discipline. The twelve steps are what can be considered as an owner's manual. The alcoholic that has the twelve steps in their lives, actually own a manual that tells them how to live. This manual tells the alcoholic to be honest, to live by the golden rule, i.e., "Do unto others as you would have them do unto you." Some of the points that are a guide to a happy and prosperous life that are listed in the manual are to first of all make amends for wrongs done in the past. This is very freeing emotionally. The alcoholic while drinking did and said a lot of things w that they are sober are remorseful. This guilt and remorse often is what keeps the alcoholic/addict still using even though everything in sight points to the fact that they should quit. By making amends, this guilt and remorse is often discarded. Not only is making amends freeing emotionally, but it allows the alcoholic to unload the baggage that they have been carrying around all of these years. This baggage has become a tremendous burden. In many cases, it has been too much of a burden to bear. This baggage has caused many alcoholics, that are still drinking to commit suicide. Because after a period of time, the alcohol stops working, that is it stops deadening the pain of the emotional baggage. At this point, the pain becomes unbearable and the only solution that the alcoholic knows is to commit suicide. Many alcoholics commit suicide in sobriety merely because they don't incorporate the owner's manual in their lives

The twelve steps also insists that the alcoholic admits when they are wrong, which is almost always. It is no longer acceptable to go around blaming others for the problems that the alcoholic has committed and caused himself. The twelve steps allow the alcoholic to confront this rationalization in the very beginning. Admitting when he is wrong allows the alcoholic to take responsibility for himself. This takes him out of the victim role and allows him to stand up and be proud. There is a quote that reads "By admitting we are wrong allows us to change because we learn from our mistakes. If we don't ever admit that we are wrong we don't allow ourselves the opportunity to learn and change. This is where the alcoholic learns to stop doing the things that will cause he and others pain. This is what is meant by getting rid of character defects.

The most important thing that the twelve steps do is emphasize spirituality. The steps constantly insist that the alcoholic find a power that is greater than himself. Because once this power is found the solution is found. It is the higher power that takes away the drink problem and allows the alcoholic to walk the streets a free man, not in bondage or enslaved to alcohol. In fact that is what the whole purpose in life is. The whole purpose of the steps , the meetings, the fellowship, and the literature of Alcoholics Anonymous, all have one goal. "That is to find a power greater than ourselves." Once this power is found, then the search is over. The answer to the drink and dope problem is found. Those character defects that were driving the alcoholic completely insane are suddenly none existent. There is no more money to make, no more riddles to solve, no more battles to win, no more mountains to climb, no more prejudges to overcome. Carl Jung knew this. That is why when Bill Wilson began to come to and realized that the program of Alcoholic's Anonymous was working, he contacted Carl Jung and commended him for having the foresight and insight to recognize that the alcoholic's problem centered in "lack of power" or lack of spirituality. In the Lord's prayer, the last line that is said says "For thine is the power, forever and ever, amen, because, that my friend is where the power lies. In fact it is said that the cure for aids may even lie in those twelve steps. The twelve steps may provide the missing link or .the missing ingredient for the cure for aids. That my friend is worth looking into . Once this power is found a whole new world opens up and yes there is **"TANGU". "TANGU"** is an

African word that means a "New Beginning." A new way of life opens up. Because of this new outlook, new ideas begin to crop up. The person begins to talk and think differently. The twelve steps enhance some of the basic principles of life such as autonomy and responsibility for self. It is very difficult to talk about a higher power without mentioning the word grace. Grace is described in Webster's unabridged dictionary to mean "Kindness". Yes, there is kindness in life. The twelve steps reminds us and stresses the point that there is divine kindness in the Universe for everyone. This gives the individual hope to try and to do new things. The twelve steps stress a universal spirituality, rather than religion. Religion tends to divide. Whereas, spirituality tends to unify. The twelve steps provide a guidelines to live by. As stated in the Big Book of Alcoholic's Anonymous, "The twelve steps are a group of principles, when practiced, allow the sufferer to become happy and usefully whole."

VII

Causalities

✦

The term causalities is used here to mean things that come as a result of having the disease of addiction. As stated earlier in a previous chapter, addiction is transmitted on passed on by genes. Addiction is passed down from one generation to another by genes. In other words, addiction is genetically induced. Many of the offspring will acquire the disease of addiction. In order to acquire this disease, one has to have the necessary components. If one of these components is not present, then the individual doesn't acquire the disease. In other words one has to have the genetic component, the biological component,. the psychological component, and the social component in order to be lucky enough to have this nightmarish <u>disease.</u> Those individuals that don't acquire the disease of addiction from their parents who are addicted acquire other mental disorders. These mental disorders are a result of addiction/alcoholism. Imagine for a moment that addiction is similar to a tree. This tree has branches. Studies have shown that children of addictive parents will many times present with "ADHD". ADHD is an abbreviation for Attention Deficit Hyperactivity Disorder. According to the DM-1V "The essential feature of Attention-Deficit/Hyperactivity Disorder is a persistent pattern of inattention and/ or hyperactivity that is more frequent and sever than is typically observed in individuals at a comparable level of development. In-attention may be manifest in academic, occupational, or social situations. Individuals with this disorder may fail to give close attention to details or may make careless mistakes in schoolwork or other tasks. Work is often messy and performed carelessly an d without considered thought. Individuals often have difficulty sustaining attention in tasks or ply activities and find it hard to persist with tasks until completion. They often appear as if their mind is elsewhere or as if they are not listening or did not hear that has just been said. They often do not follow through on instructions and fail to complete schoolwork.

Depression is another one of these branches that actually stem from the roots of alcoholism. It has been found and studies indicate that depression is genetically found

families that have a history of alcoholism. It is rarely found in families where alcoholism does not exist. Many of the offspring of the alcoholic will actually acquire the disease of alcoholism. However, many of other sibling will be diagnosed with chronic depression. Major depressive disorder may begin at any age. Some people have isolated episodes as they grow older. Some evidence suggests that 50%-60% of individuals with Major Depressive Disorder, Single Episode, can be expected to have a second episode. Major Depressive Disorder is 5-3 times more common among first degree biological relatives of persons with this disorder than among the general population. There is evidence for an increased risk of Alcohol Dependence in adult first-degreebiological relatives and there may be an increased incidence of Attention-Deficit/Hyperactivity

Disorder in children of adults with t-QCs" disorder. Bipolar disorder is also found in families of substance abuse. Approximately 10%-15% of adolescents with recurrent Major Depressive Episodes will go on to develop Bipolar 1 disorder. Completed suicide occurs in 10%-15% of individuals with Bipolar 1 Disorder. Child abuse, spouse abuse, or other violent behavior may occur during severe Manic Episodes or during those with psychotic features. Other associated problems include school truancy, school failure, occupational failure, divorce, or episodic antisocial behavior. Other associated mental disorders include Anorexi Nervosa, Bulimia Nervosa, Attention-Deficit/Hyperactivity Disorder, Panic Disorder, Social Phobia, Substance related disorders.

Schizophrenia also is believed to be one of the branches that stems from alcoholism. Schizophrenia is defined by Webster as being a psychotic disorder characterized by loss of contact with environment and by disintegration of personality. Schizophrenia is also genetically induced. It usually runs in families. The manner in which a schizophrenic child is produced is by growing up in a very dysfunctional home that is chaotic and where there are no boundaries. Individuals usually marry other individuals that are on the same emotional level. This person that is reared in a dysfunctional home marries some one that is reared in an equally disturbed dysfunctional home. These two people bring all of this dysfunction into the home and as a result the home is even more dysfunctional than the home that they grew up in. These two people produce an even more disturbed person that grows up in this dysfunctional home. This person chooses someone that is equally as disturbed. They produce a child that is even more disturbed as a result of being in this very, very dysfunctional environment. This continues and eventually a schizophrenic child is produced. Schizophrenia is related to alcoholism in that in these dysfunctional homes is present alcohol. The people producing the schizophrenic child usually are alcoholic or come from a family that has a history of alcoholism. Some offspring will develop chronic alcoholism. Those that do not will sometimes develop schizophrenia.

There are some forms of Alzheimer's disease that are directly related to alcoholism. In cases where an individual drank over a long period of time. Alcohol is an intoxicant. Intoxicant means poison. Alcohol is poison to the cells of the body. That means that alcohol kills or destroys the cells in the body. Some of these cells consist of the cells in the brain. The body has a means of creating what is known as homeostasis. Homeostasis means a balance. In other words according to Newton's first law of physics "For every action there is an opposite reaction". For example, the body takes in oxygen and gives off carbon dioxide as a means of creating homeostasis or a balance. The more alcohol or mood altering substances that are taken in the more brain cells that are destroyed. The more brain cells that are destroyed the less cognition that the person has a result. This pattern continues and over a period of time the person develops what is known as Alzheimer's disease.

Research has proven time and time again that alcohol is also related to learning disabilities. Many children of alcoholic parents develop learning disabilities such as dyslexia. Faulty patterns in the parents brain is sometimes passed on to the offspring. This many times results in learning disabilities. It is not surprising that dyslexia appears more in families with a history of alcoholism than in families of the general population.

Alcohol is the culprit that causes many of the mental disorders that are identified in the DSM-IV-R (Diagnostic Statistical Manual). Eradicating alcoholism would eliminate many of the problems that are present today that center around mental illness.

VIII

Origins Of Addiction

✦

This particular chapter will deal with what actually creates the addiction in the first place. There are many principles that will be explored concerning the origins of addiction. The first, is that alcohol and drugs are foreign substances to the human body. Alcohol is an intoxicant. In the word intoxicant we find the work toxic. Toxic "means" poison. This means that alcohol is toxic or poison to the cells of the body. The cells in the human body are very fragile and gentle. Alcohol is toxic or poison to these fragile, gentle cells. As the alcoholic progresses in his disease, he begins to pour more and more alcohol over these fragile cells. The cell membrane begins to toughen in order to be destroyed by this poisonous chemical. The cell membrane begins to become tougher and tougher as the alcoholic drinks more and more. The cell membrane begins to change its texture to accommodate this onslaught of alcohol that the alcoholic is pouring over them. The cells become hard and rigid after a period of time. Once the alcoholic becomes addicted he cannot stop drinking because if he does the cells in his body begin to cry out for alcohol. The cells in the alcoholic's body have gotten used to the alcohol being poured into them. The cells begin to cry out for alcohol because they have changed their shape to accommodate the alcohol. As a result the alcoholic's blood pressure goes up, insomnia sets in and the body temperature goes up. In other words the body goes into withdrawal because the cells are not receiving this massive amount of alcohol. Therefore the alcoholic continues drinking to avoid this phenomenon of withdrawal. This is one means of how the addiction develops.

IX

Relapse

✦

Relapse is a big part of the disease of alcoholism. The relapse rate is very high in the disease of alcoholism. Only one out of 32 individuals can stay sober. The primary reason that the relapse rate is so high is that many individuals that have the disease of alcoholism don't believe that they have a disease that is characterized by the inability to not even to take one drink, without becoming addicted all over again. The alcoholic has what is known as the alcoholic mind. That is to say that the alcoholic has many resentments that have not been resolved. There are many secrets that the alcoholic has kept bottled up inside of himself, that he has vowed to tell no one. "No one must know". The alcoholic holds on to these secrets and many times drinks over them after a long period of sobriety.

One point that is needed to be stressed here is that once a person starts the journey of sobriety, if they are going to relapse at all, it is best to have those relapses during the years or year of sobriety. The reason for that is that if the relapse is after the first year of sobriety, the person rarely gets sober and stays sober. What will usually happen if a person relapses after a long, period of sobriety, is that the person will g pt a week, a month~ two months maybe even six months but then they usually relapse all over again. There is a slogan in the Big Book that states "Over any considerable period we get worse never better." That means that as time goes on the alcoholic is "worse off" in terms of relapsing than he or she was before they ever started the recovery process.

Statistics show that there are many people that relapse after long periods of sobriety. Seldom do these people ever get sober for any length or considerable period of time. Primarily because there is the guilt and the remorse of having accumulated a considerable amount of clean time and then blowing it by relapsing. Many times this guilt and remorse causes a person to relapse time and time again.

Suicide is also associated a great deal with relapse. Rather than face the shame, ridicule, disgust, and embarrassment that goes along with relapse, many times the person that relapses gives up and decides to end it all. There are more suicides associated with the disease of alcoholism than in any other disease or disorder. In the next preceding paragraphs, we will look at what causes a person to relapse after many good solid years of sobriety.

Complacency is what causes relapse more than any other factor that exists. The person that is recovering begins to get his or her life back together again. This person's life many times has been shattered and destroyed in every way possible before the person started the process of recovery. Now, relationships have begun to be repaired. The credit has been restored. The career is back on track. People are beginning to respect the recovering person again. Last, but not least the recovering person has begun to respect himself again. He can smile as he looks into the mirror. He suddenly says to himself "Maybe, I have been making to big of a deal out going to these meetings.

I am really not that bad. Suddenly, the drink doesn't seem to be that big of a deal anymore. It is in this stage of recovery that the person becomes very vulnerable to relapse. Next relapse warning signs begin to develop.

Some of these relapse warning signs are:

1. Stopped going to meetings- The primary reason for relapse is that the person recovering person stops going to meetings. In almost every case of relapse that I have clinically interviewed. The person that has relapsed has almost consistently said that they stopped going to meetings prior to relapsing. The meetings are so important primarily because when one goes to meetings, they are reminded of how it was when they were drinking. They remember how bad it was. When one stops going to meetings they forget the devastation in their lives that was done by alcohol. The meetings remind them of just how powerless they are over alcohol. Secondly, when one stops going to meetings they miss a very important part of recovery that only the meetings can provide. As stated earlier in the book, alcoholism is a relapsing disease. People are constantly relapsing. Statistics are that only 1 out of 32 people that try to stop drinking are actually able to stop drinking. The rest are constantly relapsing. The most important part about going to meetings is that these people that relapse come back to the meetings and talk about their relapse. They tell o the devastation and how awful it was to relapse. The pain that they are feeling is quite apparent. While sitting in the meeting, one hears and sees what happens to people when they relapse. Suddenly the drink doesn't look so good. The thought of drinking doesn't seem like such a good idea because the recovering person remembers what happened to them when they were drinking. They remember

the pain and the feelings of hopelessness that were brought on when they last drank. If a person stops going to meetings then they won't see the results of what happens when a person relapses and they pick up the drink up again.

2. Complacency-this is when the person begins to feel better. Some of the devastation of drinking for many, many, years has begun to repair and the person begins to feel that he or she really are not alcoholic and that it is possible to drink again first drink. This is known as "Stinking Thinking".

3. The person's life becomes very busy and suddenly they stop going to meetings. The meetings begin to get in the way of other engagements. These other engagements are sometimes centered around business, relationships, or school. Missing meetings is very dangerous because the meetings is what reminds the person how important that it is not to take the first drink.

4. The person begins to feel sorry for him or herself. The "poor me's" begin to become a part of the person's thinking pattern. A mild form of depression develops. This depression is similar to dysthymia. Underneath the person feels that the bottom is going to fall out any day. There is this sense of impending doom that develops.

5. The person begins to hang around old drinking girlfriends or boyfriends. They begin hanging around old play grounds and playmates more and less around the AA program. The human being is a creature of habit. "Piaget" called it modeling. In other words association brings assimililation. If the person hangs around sober people that makes the person want to be and get sober. If the person hangs around drinking and using people that

6. Romancing- this is when the person begins to think about how much fun that was had while using. This person has forgotten all about the pain, remorse, suffering, powerlessness, devastation, destruction, and or total annihilation that has taken place in- all arrears ' of life as a result of using and drinking. The thoughts of how drinking has made one's life almost unbearable and how death had become a welcoming thought as a result of using has suddenly been forgotten. These thoughts have been replaced by wanting and needing relief by using and drinking.

7. Feelings of control- the person begins to think that they have control of their life again. This person suddenly begins to think that they can't control using or drinking. These thoughts are ridiculous. As was stated earlier, once a person loses control, they never, never, never, never, regain control. Total abstinence is necessary to recover from an addiction. Promises to cut down are promises that cannot be kept. Any use will keep the addiction active. Abstinence is a necessary first step.

8. Substitution- This is when a person begins to think that since they obviously were addicted to one drug and not to another that it is possible to use the other drug in moderation. For example, if a person or individual feels good even when something is terribly wrong. Let's say a person was to lose their particular job. This person would naturally begin to feel very bad and even depressed. The brain begins naturally to secret this dopamine that calms the person down and ultimately makes the person not kill themselves. When a person drinks this same dopamine is released. This is the mechanism that makes the person feel good. Each person has their preferred drug or (DOC)· drug of choice. The reason that it is the

drug of choice is that it causes the most dopamine to be released. For some this DOC is alcohol. For others it is cocaine. For others it is speed, marijuana, barbiturates, heroin, and the like.

9. Therefore even if the person changes drugs, for a short period, they will still revert back to their drug of choice because this is the drug that causes the dopamine to be released in large molecules. This explains why a person that was addicted to cocaine that begins drinking alcohol soon start looking for their drug of choice. They revert back to the cocaine because they want that rush that they get from the cocaine
The cocaine causes more dopamine to be released in a much more rapid pace. The dopamine floods the brain and this is what makes the person feel good. The alcohol is a much more slower gradual process. The substituted drug does not cause the magic to happen in the brain that the (DOC) drug of choice does. This is the reason that the addict must remain completely abstinent. There is no in between. Either the person is going to be actively using or completely drug free.

X

Hitting Bottom

✦

Hitting bottom is a very crucial stage in recovery. A person usually doesn't begin to get sober until they have truly hit bottom. The harder the bottom, the better the chances are of recovery. What is "Hitting bottom"? Hitting bottom is literally when a person is brought to their knees. This is usually the lowest point in a person's life where a person feels ultimate despair as result of drinking and using mind altering chemicals. A bottom can consist of a financial as well as an emotional bottom. Either one or both can occur to cause a person to hit bottom. When one hits bottom there is usually a very deep depression that sits in. During these times of depression individuals often think about committing suicide. Hitting bottom can be compared to the analogy of "It feels like it is raining bricks everyday." That is to say that anything that can go wrong usually does. There doesn't seem to be any end to the hopelessness and devastation that takes place when a person is hitting bottom. What is usually very difficult is to allow the person to hit his or her bottom without attempting to rescue them. Many times more harm than good is done when a person attempts to rescue a person from the consequences that come as a result of using mind altering chemicals. The person usually doesn't recover until the people around him or her become fed up and stop coming to the person's rescue. At this point, and only at this point is there a chance of recovery. The family members must set very strict boundaries or limits with the person that is using. These boundaries may seem harsh and unfair to the person that is still using. However, it is what the person needs in order to recover. Many people die from this awful malady because their love ones rescued them and did not allow them to truly hit the bottom that they had created for themselves. An example of this can be Elvis Pressley. The people around this beloved man kept covering for him and doing him favors that they allowed him to die. In essence it can be said that They loved him too much.

Hitting bottom comes when there is no where else to turn. The Big Book of Alcoholic's anonymous describes it this way. "There were but two choices. That is to continue on using until the bitter end or give up and live a life based on spiritual principles." In other words when a person hits bottom they either get sober or die a very sad death that comes as a result of drinking or using mind altering chemicals. Usually the sooner that a person is allowed to hit bottom, the better off they are. Hitting bottom usually consists of legal problems, family problems, financial problems, employment problems, relationship problems, feelings of loneliness, hopelessness, and the inability to communicate with others. As stated earlier the bottom can consist of one of the above or combination or all of the above. There are two types of bottoms. There is what can be considered a "High bottom". This is the person that has not completely lost his job, finances, relationships, employment and still may be functioning well in the eyes of society. Low bottoms are those who have lost it all. These people do have the job problems, relationship problems, financial problems, bankruptcies, legal problems, facing jail or strict sever legal consequences. It should be pointed out however that when a person first gets sober, no matter how low their particular bottom is, because of the denial factor of the disease these people believe they are high bottom drunks even though they may be practically homeless. After they are sober for a while, they begin to see how low their particular bottom was. It should be pointed out however that the lower a person's bottom is not directly proportional to success rate of recovery. This is evidenced by the fact that the union missions are full of people that have had as low of a bottom as one can imagine. However these people very seldom get sober. Whereas one can attend some Alcoholic's Anonymous meetings and see Jaguars, Mercedes Benz's, Ferrari's and the like parked outside. These people were able to get sober even though they did not end up homeless or in prison. These people probably have had an emotional bottom which can be just as horrible as a physical bottom. In some cases it is even worse. There is no hard and fast rule of who will get sober and who won't. However, it can be safe to say that the more consequences that a person has in their lives when they hit bottom, the better the chances are of them getting sober. When a person hits bottom, Carl Jung referred to this as a deep depression develops. This depression is similar to a dark whole. When this happens the individual gives up his "old ideas" and is willing to try something different. At this point recovery is then considered possible.

XI

Recovery

✦

During the phase of the addicted person experiences "TANGU". **"TANGU"** is an African word that means "A new beginning". That is what recovery is for most addicts. It is a new beginning at a new way of life. The disease of alcoholism is the only disease where sublimation occurs. With most diseases when a person recovers, they just revert back to where they were before they ever got the disease. For, example if a person had rheumatism in the leg. When they recover from the rheumatism they are not able to run the hundred yard dash any faster than they were before they got the rheumatism. In other words, the other person is not any better off because they had the rheumatism. However, with the disease of addiction when a person recovers, sublimation occurs. Sublimation means that they are better after recovering than they were before they ever got the disease. The person is better spiritually, emotionally, physically, mentally, and many times financially. This is the only disease where sublimation occurs. Recovery is the most interesting and best part about the disease of alcoholism. Webster defines recovery as meaning "To get back." During the process of using and drinking, the addicted person lost a lot because they were so focused on getting their drug of choice. Nothing was important but getting that next drink or next drug. As a result many people lost their children, homes, jobs and faced financial ruin as a result of having this disease that tells the addicted person "you don't have me". Most of all the number one thing that was lost was that the person loses themselves. They lose their confidence, morals, ethics, and belief system. The addicted person finds himself in places that ordinarily he would, he goes out to find his drug of choice. He finds himself saying things that he wouldn't dream of saying if he weren't under the influence. Many recovering people say that they wish that they could take back some of the things they said while they were using. Many active users find themselves stealing from the ones they love. Therefore trust is lost. The disease becomes paramount to all other interest. At this point it begins telling the person that is actively using. You are not this. You are not that. You will never amount to anything. Look at how much better off everyone else is except you. Over time and over a period of years, the addicted person begins to lose their confidence and hope. Where once was seen a thriving prosperous person. Now all that is seen is a weakling, smelly, person with their head between their legs. The addicted person begins to be very mean to the people that are the closest to them. The addict begins to push love ones away. The addict stops attending family functions because they do not want others to see how low they have sunk. They push people away so that the addict can continue drinking and using without anyone around to stop them. Many relationships are lost because of this phenomenon. When one starts to recover the old self dies. The new self emerges. As is stated in St. Francis prayer, "It is by dying that one awakens to Eternal Life."

Recovery means to get back into the main stream of life. In a book by Robert B. Ewen, Personality Theories Abraham

Mazlow said in his "Hierarchy of Needs" that the number one cause of neurosis or psychiatric problems is that the person is not allowed to self-actualize or reach their goals.

Abraham Mazlow's HierArchy of Needs Diagram.

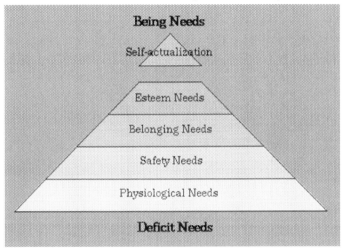

The self-actualization diagram can be used to describe addiction and recovery. When a person is actively using they go down the self-actualization diagram from top to bottom. The first thing that is given up on is their goals. The addiction is so paramount or prevalent that goals become of least importance. The confidence level is way down and the goals are soon forgotten about.

The next thing to go is the esteem needs. These are things that are done so that the person will feel good about themselves. This is when the person strives to attain respect from others. This makes one feel good about themselves. This includes, dressing properly, proper etiquette, proper diction and the like. Well, in active addiction these things are less important. Getting the drug or drink is much more important. As the self-esteem begins to erode or evaporate the addict begins to dislike himself and ceases to love himself. In order to love someone else it is first very important and vital that one first loves himself. The next stage to disintegrate is the Belonging and love needs. The addict is in love with his drug of choice and finds it very difficult to find time to love someone else. Getting the drug of choice becomes more important than having people to love. The next need to evaporate is the Safety needs. Safety needs involve having shelter and a place that is safe to store goods as well as to rest. When one is actively using, the rent doesn't get paid. Therefore, one becomes homeless. Although, not all, but a large percentage of the people that are homeless are that way because they made a conscious decision to drink or use drugs rather than spend the money on shelter.

The next need to go is the physiological needs. The physiological needs involve hunger, thirst, sex, oxygen, sleep and the elimination of bodily waste. This is the very

last need to go when a person is actively drinking or using drugs. This is according to the hierarchy of needs diagram. It is quite obvious why this would be the very last need to go. One needs these physiological needs in order to stay alive. However as the disease progresses, the physiological needs become less important. Getting the drink or drug is paramount to all other interest. It is not uncommon to hear of someone actively using to break off their tooth to get drugs from the dentist. Many alcoholics die of malnutrition because they choose to buy cheap wine rather than food, which their bodies desperately need in order to stay alive. The road to recovery is in the opposite direction of the Hierarchy of Needs in the diagram. Recovery starts from the bottom up. The first need to be affected is the Physiological Need. When a person starts to recover they are first concerned with eating and taking care of themselves. For example a person that is not drinking would be more aware of the fact that they are starving. A starving person cares little about writing majestic poetry or buying an expensive car. The road to recovery takes on the opposite direction of the Hierarchy of Needs in the diagram. Recovery starts from the bottom up. The first need to be affected is the Physiological Need. When a person starts to recovery they are first concerned with eating and taking care of themselves. For example, a person that is not drinking would be more aware of the fact that they are starving. A starving person cares little about writing majestic poetry, buying an impressive-looking car, finding a sweetheart, or carefully avoiding the possibility of injury-or anything other than the over-riding goal of obtaining food. The recovering person is more concerned with fulfilling the physiological needs. They begin doing this by first getting a job. The job supplies the money necessary to buy food, get dental care, medical care, and the like.

After the physiological needs become increasingly satisfied, the recovering person next becomes concerned with the safety needs. The next hierarchy gradually emerges as a motivator. These safety needs involve the quest for an environment that is stable, predictable, and free from anxiety and chaos. The recovering person will look for a nice apartment, a home to rent, and eventually buying a low cost home. Many recovering people that were once homeless now own their own homes.

Once the safety needs are met, that is after the recovering person begins to work and meet his or her physiological needs, they acquire shelter. After acquiring shelter, they begin to look around for someone to share all of this material that they have acquired. They begin to look for someone to love. Abraham Mazlow said that human beings are social animals. That is to say that they need someone to belong to.

After the belonging need is met. The next need is very vital and important to the recovering person. That is the Esteem Need. This is where the person begins doing something that will ultimately improve their self-esteem and make them feel good about themselves. Many people elect to return back to school and get the degree that they dreamed about while they were drinking. Mazlow cautions that true self-esteem is based on real competence and significant achievement, rather than external fame and unwarranted adulation. Many recovering addicts write books, paint, do sculpture and the like. These are things that build self-esteem and allow the person to feel good about themselves.

The last need that is at the top of the Hierarchy of Human Needs is the need to self-actualize. The highest form of need is self-actualization, which consists of discovering and fulfilling one's own innate potentials and capacities. Self-actualization is idiosyncratic, since every person is different. The individual [must do] what he, individually is fitted for. A musician must make music. An artist must paint. A poet must write, if he is to be ultimately at peace with himself.

Thus self-actualization is a growth motive similar to actualization in Rogerian theory, except that it does not become important (or even noticeable) until the physiological, safety, love, and esteem needs have been at least partially satisfied. Like Jungian individuation, therefore, self-actualization is prominent only in older people. Those individuals that are recovering many times do reach their goals, and reach their full potential. They do get a chance to self-actualize.

Because many individuals find themselves in precarious situations in which they are not allowed to reach their full potential or self-actualize, these individuals often times turn to drugs and alcohol to cope with not being allowed to self-actualize. For example, if someone's goal was to become doctor, and they found themselves married with four children to feed. It would become very difficult to self-actualize or to reach their goal. This person may turn to alcohol to cope with this inability to self-actualize. Another example could be that if a woman had aspirations of going to college to pursue her academic goals, suddenly became pregnant and she didn't believe in abortion. If this woman found herself married and raising a family, she may turn to addictive prescription pills to cope with this set back. It is believed that self-actualization is very important when looking at addiction. It is not uncommon for recovering people to be called late-bloomers because they don't start careers until late in life. They still have the need to self-actualize and many times don't carryout this need until they are older. Once they self-actualize, however, the need to drink and do drugs is no longer present. Looking at ways and means to allow individuals to self-actualize could be explored further in reference to treating individuals addicted to substances. One may need to be married and have children to self-actualize. One may need to work for themselves to self-actualize. One may need to volunteer more to feed the hungry and to house the homeless in order to self-actualize.

Recovery is the process of discovering oneself. While a person is drinking, he or she really doesn't know themselves because they have been drunk for so many years. Recovery is the process of discarding the old and visiting the new. St. Francis said it is through dying that we get a chance to live. The old drunk person dies and a new vibrant person that is full of life emerges. It is similar to the ship the phoenix. The Phoenix sunk. And up came this beautiful bird out of the water.

Recovery is about peeling back the onion layers until one gets to their true self. Chuck Chamberlain describes it as uncovering, discovering, and discarding. Once the true self emerges. The person begins liking himself again. The self-esteem rises and the person doesn't find it necessary to drink again. However, it is very important to change the playmates and playgrounds. It is strongly recommended that no alcohol or any kind of drug that will trigger alcoholism be kept in the home. Relapse prevention is basically a process of behavioral change.

An important fact to remember is that addiction is disease that is treatable. Unlike ids, which has no successful recoveries. There are literally hundreds of thousands of people living happy recoveries from alcoholism.

In order to get into recovery, usually people receive counseling. Here we look at how different counseling techniques can be used to get a person into treatment and in essence break through the denial.

A.   1. The first counseling technique that will be looked at is RET. RET is an abbreviation for Rational Emotive Therapy. This counseling technique was developed by a Psychologist by the name of Albert Ellis. Ellis says that it is the belief system that has to be changed in order. o change the behavior. Ellis goes on to say that is this faulty belief system that causes neurosis, psychosis, mental illness, and alcoholism. This therapy is based on the first five letters of the alphabet. These are A,B,C,D, and E. A is the activating event. The activating event is the precipitating factor that causes the discomfort. Example is " My girlfriend left." or "I lost my job.

B= Belief system. My belief system says now that my girlfriend has gone, I will never find another one. Therefore I will be lonely the rest of my life. This type of thinking is what keeps one drinking. The person drinks in order to deal with this conflict. However once the belief system is changed to: Yes it is true that my girlfriend is gone but however half of the population is made of women so chances are pretty good that I will have another girlfriend. The person doesn't need to drink because there is no conflict now to resolve. One that is heavily addicted to a substance typically has many false beliefs that have to be restructured. The cognition skills or thinking process has to be changed many, times.

2. **PSYCHOANALYTIC** - Proponents of a psycho-dynamic perspective view alcoholism as unfulfilled needs and the ways that alcoholics learned to satisfy such needs during their early stages of development. For example, one psychodynamic theory proposes that alcoholism is the result of fixation at the oral

stage for psychosexual development in which discomfort is reduced through oral behaviors. Thus, the alcoholic uses an oral behavior (drinking) to reduce stress. Another psychodynamic theory postulates that alcohol is used as a means of achieving a sense of power. From this point of view, the alcoholic is seen as unable to satisfy his/her need for power in "reality" and therefore, uses alcohol to support his/her fantasy of importance. Primarily the Psychoanalytic or psychodynamic approach involves unearthing deep seeded secrets that have been repressed because they have been too painful and to conflict laden for the conscious to deal with. These painful thoughts have been pushed down to the subconscious where they lie. Each time these thoughts start to surface the addicted person uses substances to push the thoughts back down. Many times these thoughts are centered around sexual abuse or some other very emotional act such as verbal abuse, and physical abuse. Perhaps there was some trauma such as some type of post traumatic stress that has been repressed. Such as seeing a violent act that happened to a close relative. The psychoanalytic approach is about getting to the core root of these painful conflict laden areas, unearthing them, getting them up, and talking about them. At this point a catharsis occurs or healing and the person no longer finds it necessary to drink over these things. The psychoanalytic approach is very effective.

3. Transactional Analysis Theory - Transactional Analysis (TA) was developed by Eric Berne. This therapy is based on the notions that (1) each individual possesses three ego states (Parent, Adult, and Child), (2) each individual follows a fife "script" or plan established during his/her childhood and representing the

basic views about him/herself and others, and (3) individuals engage in "games" which advance their life scripts. :

. the "drunk and proud of it" game in which the alcoholic is attempting to "get even" with domineering people in his/her life (e.g. parent, spouse).

. The "lush" game in which the alcoholic drinks in response to defects in emotional and social support, i.e. in order to receive "strokes" (e.g., by obtaining love through being "rescued")

. The "wino" game in which the alcoholic uses the disease concept of alcoholism to justify his\ her drinking (e.g., "I am sick and can't control my drinking") and to get others to take care of him or her. An important contribution of the TA model of alcoholism is its recognition of the role of other, especially family members, in creating or sustaining the alcoholic's drinking behavior. When the role of the family is recognized, treatment is aimed at reversing the alcoholic's games by involving all individuals involved in them (significant others").

4. Behavioral/learning Theory: Like psychodynamic theories of alcoholism reject the notion of alcoholism as a disease. They instead view abusive drinking as a learned behavior. Proponents of the learning perspective emphasize the rewarding aspects of drinking; e.g., tension-reduction, enhancement of social relationships, peer approval, feelings of personal power and euphoria, and the association of drinking with adult status or masculinity.

According to this view, alcohol use is activated whenever the alcoholic, is faced with certain critical internal or environmental cues. This notion implies that alcoholism may start as a symptom of an underlying disorder which induces the learning of the alcoholism pattern. Once the pattern is continued, the alcoholism may persist even when the original underlying cause is absent. The learned response of excessive drinking is maintained when physical dependence develops and continued consumption of alcohol allows the alcoholic to avoid the negative consequences associated with non-drinking (e.g., withdrawal symptoms).

XII

Treatment

✦

Treatment of alcoholism is based on the behavioral learning theory using operant conditioning. Using this approach treatment of alcoholism is based on rewards. When one relapses or doesn't obey suggestions, there are consequences. Sobriety should be measured in increments of 30 days. At the end of each thirty days a person is commended and given a token. This concept is based on collecting the tokens. A person's merit is based on how many tokens that they are able to collect. Tokens serve as a marker for the amount of sobriety that one has achieved. After collecting the tokens over a length of time. A person soon has accumulated a great deal of sobriety. The goal of collecting the tokens is to get to a years sobriety. Once a year of sobriety is achieved, then the person has a good chance of remaining sober. Statistics show that if a person is able to achieve a year of sobriety, they have an excellent chance of remaining sober. Physically, it takes about a year to completely get the alcohol out of the human body. Once the alcohol is completely out of the body, the cravings begin to subside and become much less. The goal of behavioral technique of picking up tokens is to get to a year. This procedure works. The AA sobriety approach is based on this method.

Bandura said that the main way to change behavior is through modelling. He did a study that demonstrated that once a behavior is modelled, the behavior will be learned regardless if there is reinforcement or not. He worked with apes. He showed that if the ape played with a doll in a nice passive way, the children watching this played with the same doll in a nice passive way. He also observed that if the ape played with the doll in an aggressive way the children played with the doll in an aggressive way.

Therefore using the behavioral/modeling approach, this approach is based on choosing people that have abstained for a period of time, and doing exactly what they are doing. This means doing whatever the person that has been sober for a while is doing to maintain sobriety. This approach is very effective.

As was pointed out earlier, AA uses this same approach to get members sober. Each time a person goes to a meeting they are able to see other people that have successfully stayed sober. This reinforces that it is possible to get and stay sober. Modeling is very effective in changing behavior in treatment.

5. Gestalt Therapy- This form of therapy involves confrontation and helping the addicted person break through the wall of denial. Denial is not a river in Egypt. Denial is what keeps the addicted person using and doesn't allow the person to see the truth. Confrontation is used when a person contradicts themselves and when the person doesn't see how the consequences that they are facing are the result of their behavior. This form of therapy is also referred to as "putting a person in the hot seat". This therapy is very effective. Gestalt therapy also involves "The Empty chair". This involves role playing situations that are difficult to handle and usually end

up with the person using their particular drug of choice. For example a person would role play how they would handle running into their old using buddies. Gestalt therapy was made popular by Fritz Perls. He did a great deal of work with psychodrama. Psychodrama is very similar to role-playing. This involves working through very difficult situations that are conflict laden by role playing the particular situation. Gestalt therapy is famous for getting the person to stay in the "here and now". Perlz formulated that it is when a person focuses on the past or the future that psychic conflict sets up that causes a person to drink or use. Therefore the key is getting the person to stay in the "Now".

XIII

Summary

✦

What is it that makes recovery possible from the disease of alcoholism. The most effective method proven so far that has allowed individuals to recover in mass has been AA. (Alcoholic's Anonymous) The Preamble from Alcoholic's Anonymous reads tells exactly what Alcoholic's Anonymous is: Alcoholic's Anonymous is a fellowship of men and women who share their experience strength and hope one with each other that they may solve their common problem and help others to recover from alcoholism

The only requirement for AA membership is a desire to stop drinking. There are no dues or fees for AA membership; we are self-supporting through our own contributions. AA is not allied with any sect, denomination, politics, organization, or institution; does not wish to engage in any controversy; neither endorses or opposes any causes. Our primary purpose is to stay sober and help other alcoholics achieve sobriety. [Copyright and printed by permission of A.A. Grapevine,Inc.]

This is the backbone of AA. But what is it that makes AA successful when so many other organization3such as the Washingtonians, The Women's Suffrage movement of the early 1900's, and organized religion per se- have all failed. It is in the fact that AA is based on the 12 steps. There is something spiritual about the word 12. There are 12 months in the year. There were 12 disciples. There are Twelve Traditions. In Waikiki, Honolulu, there is an AA meeting on the beach. That is not so significant. What is significant is that the meeting takes place under 12 coconut trees that are in a symmetric circle. Those coconut trees were there in that same position even before AA got started. What is even more impressive is that right beside these 12 coconut trees that are in a circle is; there are 6 coconut trees that are in a symmetric circle. AA history says that at first there were 6 steps and later Bill Wilson one of the Co-founders of AA developed them into 12. Both of these groups of trees were there in that same shape before AA was even dreamed of. That my friend is one of the reasons that makes one believe there is something spiritual about AA. AA is the only proven method for getting alcoholics sober.

Addiction is a spiritual disease that requires a spiritual answer. Addiction is a disease that is multifactorial. That is to say that there are many factors that cause the disease, not just one. When the spiritual piece is put in place, positive results are given. There has not been any significant progress made in the attempt to find cure for aids. This is due to the fact that there has not been an attempt made that incorporates a spiritual answer. The modalities that are being researched are based on a medical model. There needs to be an attempt made that includes a medical, psychological, as well as and most importantly, a spiritual model. After all, from the beginning of time, and not until the last 60 years, there was no effective treatment for addiction including alcoholism. There were many different attempts made to alcoholism and other addictions, but no treatment was successful. It wasn't until a stockbroker by the name of Bill Wilson and Proctologist by the name of Robert Smith met and formed Alcoholic's Anonymous that people have been able to live happy, useful, and prosperous lives. The model consists of medical (if the person needs detoxing), psychological, and spiritual approaches.

SELF-SERVING DIATRIBE-NICOTINE

It would be almost impossible to cover the subject of addiction without discussing Nicotine. On August 27,1996, President Clinton signed a bill that would identify nicotine as an addictive drug that should be regulated. There are some studies that indicate that nicotine is more addictive than heroin. More deaths are caused by nicotine and are nicotine related than by any other drug.

What seems ludicrous to me and almost preposterous is that there are all these laws and regulations prohibiting the sale and distribution of illicit drugs. Many class- 1V drugs such as codeine cough syrup is kept behind the counter of pharmacies and is only sold in many cases by a prescription from a licensed physician or is signed out by the person buying the class-1V cough syrup. However, nicotine has proven to be much more harmful to the body than class-1V cough syrup, but hardly anything is done to regulate it. Consider this fact. Most people who smoke cigarettes start to smoke in their teenage years. These are the formative years, when one is vulnerable to almost any suggestion. The teenagers start to smoke many times because the cigarettes are so readily available. Before they know it, they are hooked, because the drug is so addictive. There is hardly any safeguard in place that would discourage or prohibit a teenager from smoking cigarettes. Cigarettes are readily available without too much trouble to get.

What is of greatest concern is, if there is all this concern over using drugs, and giving long sentences for selling drugs? Why in heavens name isn't something being done about the wholesale selling of cigarettes. I see people who are on the tank. These people suffer from emphysema. This is caused by a lack of oxygen. What has happened is that the tar from the cigarettes builds up in the lungs. This has made the muscles in the lungs weak. The lungs are not able to expand and contract to get oxygen. Therefore a person has to carry the tank in order to breathe. Yes, the selling of cigarettes should be regulated more tightly. Frankly, because of the excellent lobbying that the tobacco companies do, cigarette smoking will probably never decrease dramatically. Cigarette smoking is an addiction and cigarettes should be regulated just as any other drug should be regulated.

Yes, the consensus is in, alcoholism and drug addiction is a disease. There is substantial agreement in the medical, psychological, and social fields that addiction and alcoholism is psychobiological, and biopsychosocial with variations and sometimes minor deviations.

Alcoholism is a pathology or malady in its own right. That is to say that it is not a symptom of something else. The American Medical Association's interpretation of alcoholism as a disease says that "the treatment primarily involves not taking a drink. Treatment facilities report high rates of success because they primarily emphasize the importance of attendance at AA. Psycotherapy alone doesn't work because it is inherently self-defeating. If the anxiety and tension are the result of drinking are what ultimately bring alcoholics to treatment, the reduction of these may function more to sustain drinking than to promote recovery. A probing psychotherapy can be very threatening and can literally drive one to drink. After all the primary reason that most people drink is to forget these awful things. Sigmund Freud referred to this as repression. Meanwhile the patient gets sicker and sicker until the patient stops drinking. Therefore, the belief is that drinking is the problem.

The purpose here is not to unearth why people drink or even why they get drunk. Some people deliberately get drunk for a variety of reasons, but they are not alcoholics. Alcoholics can always give a reason why they drink: I worked all week, it's too hot, it's too cold, it's raining, the sun is shining, and the like. However, very few will give a reason why they can't stop drinking. The denial in them says as Marylyn Monroe once said, "I can quit if I want to. I just don't want to". The truth is that these people can't stop drinking no matter how hard they try. Without intervention it is literally impossible for this group of people to stop drinking. This intervention will involve some type of cognitive transformation that will result in a behavioral transformation. By cognitive transformation what is meant is that the thought patterns that a person has initially has to be changed. This person that was once so obsessed and dedicated to drinking now becomes obsessed and consumed with not drinking. It's similar to what happens with smoking. When a person is smoking, they really love smoking. However, when they stop smoking, they hate even the smell of cigarettes. They will have NO SMOKING signs all over the house, in the car, in the office and even complain about allowing people to smoke in a stadium. This is what happens when a person's cognitive thinking patterns or apparatus has been changed. This is what makes the etiology or what causes alcoholism or addiction so amazing. One could argue that there are socio-factors. That is to say the culture that one is raised in makes one predisposed to alcoholism and drug addiction. This may well be true however, there are many people reared in this same culture that do not every drink at all. Then there are those reared in this culture that drink very little. This makes the argument that it is the culture or the environment that predisposes one to alcoholism very weak indeed. True there are a large number of American Indians and African Americans with very high rates of alcoholism. But now there are also very large numbers of African Americans that are very successful lawyers and doctors that do not drink alcohol at all or very minimally that are reared in these same environments. This rules out the argument of alcoholism being socio-cultural. The fact that the alcohol rates are higher per capital in the African American community is not attributed to the culture. That is just like saying that the Italian culture produced the Mafia. Even further, that all Italians are prone to violence because of the Italian culture. This is not only preposterous but it is ludicrous as well. The truth is that there is a segment of the Italian culture that got involved in crime. I might add, this is a very small segment of the Italian culture.

Just as violence is not socio-cultural neither is addiction or alcoholism. Alcoholism is a disease and this has absolutely nothing to do with society or the culture that one is raised in. The fact is that one is born an alcoholic and remains alcoholic until they die. Why is this. For some questions there are no answers. Why are there fish in the ocean and birds in the sky. Why can't man fly. Why is the sky blue. Why are some people diabetic. Why are some people born with the phenomenon of craving. That is that if they take one drink. One lousy drink, they will crave alcohol and even kill for it. While others will take this same drink and not ever think of alcohol again. The trick is to recognize and realize that there are these people in the world and if you are one of them or if your love one is one of them. Then this mean that they can't drink and there is no way possible to make them so that they can drink without craving it. Once a person realizes this fact and accepts this fact then they are able to live a happy and useful lives. It is not important how the horse got in the ditch. What is important is how do we get the horse out of the ditch   It is not important How, When, or Why you or your love one started drinking but it is important for you or them to stop for various reasons. These various reasons are simple in scope. If the person doesn't stop drinking, they will end up in one of three places. These three places are jail, mental, institutions, or dead. I might add these consequences do not necessarily have to take place in this particular order. Many addicts die very horrible, tragic deaths at very early ages.

(STATISTICS ON CONSEQUENCES ON SUBSTANCE USE). (DRAW DIAGRAM DEPICTING LAW OF DIMINISHING RETURNS:

According to Dr. R.T. Ravenholt of World Health Surveys, Inc. there were approximately 100,000 deaths in 1980 attributed to directly to alcohol. Of these, 18,500 were directly related to cirrhosis to the liver or to alcohol dependency syndrome; 10,600 deaths were related to other diseases caused by alcohol; 9,200 were alcohol-caused cancers; 40,000 were accidents caused by alcohol; and 21,000 were alcohol-caused deaths by violence. Because various diseases exist at the time of death, e.g., stroke, cancer, aids, pneumonia, these illnesses are frequently listed on death certificates as the cause of death. Yet these illnesses may have taken years to develop, growing slowly, unnoticed under the steady onslaught of acetaldehyde, of alcohol. Cancers of the lips, mouth, tongue, pharynx, and esophagus occur more often in those with alcoholism than in others. Of these cancers, 34% are fatal. The chronic use of alcohol together with tobacco accounts for 75% of these cancers. Esophageal varicose veins (varicose) develop and many an alcoholic has bled to death when these veins burst. Ulcers and stomach cancer result from alcoholism, as well as irritation of the bowel.

More than 75% of cases of chronic pancreatitis in the U.S.A. occur in alcoholics. Acetaldehyde in sufficient amounts from pancreatic stones that obstruct the ducts. In a study of pancreatic cancer, 75% of the victims had a history of moderate to heavy drinking.

The first of the liver diseases to develop is alcoholic fatty liver, because alcohol replaces fat as the preferred fuel for the liver; consequently, the unburned fat builds up in the liver, increasing acid levels in the blood which are associated with hyperglycemia (elevated blood sugar).

Alcohol hepatitis is characterized by the inflammation and death of individual liver cells. This condition is painful; the person may experience nausea, jaundice, and fever. hepatitis, as well a fatty liver, are reversible.

The liver disease that develops at a later stage is known as cirrhosis. The liver is so plugged with toxic substances that blood cannot flow through and backs up. The blood, in turn, picks up these toxins and carries them to the head where they do further damage to an already damaged brain. This has been called "blood-sludge."

Scar tissue develops in the liver, further cutting off the free flow of blood vessels in the head and face to rupture. It is because of the constriction of the blood vessels to the hear that thin -walled, delicate veins of the esophagus must carry more blood to the heart.

This extra duty makes them hemorrhage, forcing the person to vomit blood. Cirrhotic liver is a major cause of death in those plagued by alcoholism. Upon autopsy, as much as 30% of alcoholics had undetected liver cancer. It is suspected that the reason that so few cirrhotics die from liver cancer is that cirrhosis develops much faster and that liver cancer has not had time to develop. Nevada, Alaska, and the District of Columbia have the highest per capita alcohol consumption; they also have the highest death rates from cirrhosis.

Cardiomyopathy is a primary cause of death in the alcoholic suffers. It is characterized by chronic shortness of breath, swelling (of hands and feet, the lungs, and the viscra), fatigue, heart palpitations, and bloodstained sputum. High blood pressure and irregular heartbeats are other signs of heart disease connected with alcoholism.

Heart disease is the number one cause of death in the United States. Many cardiac and diabetic patients are alcoholics who are being treated for heart problems and diabetes. These critical medical problems are a direct result of alcoholism, for which they are not being treated; likewise, their death certificates will not mention the root cause of death, alcoholism, but the resultant cause of their alcoholism , heart disease or diabetes.

Myopathy is a disease of the skeletal muscles, long associated with alcoholism. The muscles become weak and cramp painfully. Leg cramps at night are common among alcoholics. General muscle weakening accounts for many of the falls and mysterious bruises alcoholics suffer. For example, a college girl entered treatment because she would wake up every mourning covered with bruises. She had no idea where they came from and did not remember falling. Even when she was not drinking, her legs would give out when she least expected it.

Many alcoholics have to come to alcoholic treatment centers in wheelchairs. They have many times been in these wheelchairs many years because they actually have lost the ability to walk. What has happened the alcohol has weakened the muscles so much that, many people just continue drinking and eventually lose the use of their legs through myopathy. After being in treatment a few weeks, it is not unusual to see these same people walking, running, playing tennis, basketball and the like.

Blood disorders such as anemia and nutritional disorders of the B complex vitamins such as polyneuropathy, Werniche's encephalopathy, and Korsakoff's psychosis occur in the later stages of alcoholism. Many alcoholics simply do not eat. They get their nutrition from the alcohol, which s very limited in its nutritional properties. They get all or most of their calories from alcohol. These are empty calories, devoid of essential amino acids, vitamins, and minerals. These nutritional disorders effect the central nervous system and the brain, resulting in headaches, confusion, agitation, and hallucinations. If left untreated, irreversible brain damage (Korsakoff's psychosis results. This is known as "wet brain". Seventy to 80% of alcoholic afflicted men experience a reduction in the production of the male hormone experience an increase in the production of the female hormone estrogen, which results in the enlargement of mammary glands and a general feminization of the alcoholic man. Women, likewise experience infertility, loss of sex drive, and a loss of secondary sex characteristics such as breast and pelvic fat accumulation. Cancer of the breast is more frequent among alcoholic women. According to a 1987 study, even women who drink moderately (three drinks a week) run higher risks of breast cancer than those women who do not drink.

2.   A. Pharmacology and the Treating of Addiction-Natraxone has been effective in treating opioid addiction and alcoholism. Natraxone is effective because it blocks the opiate receptors. A good way to explain this phenomenon is that the opioid is looking for a receptor cite. In other words the opioid is looking for a date. This date is found at the receptor cite. Natraxone is standing in front of the door to the receptor cite. Therefore the opioid is not able to connect with the receptor cite because the natraxone blocks the cite. Even though a person uses opioids or alcohol, they are not able to experience a high because the natraxone blocks the receptor cite. By using natraxone, the addict is not able to get high and therefore soon stops using the substance because the needed affect is not being produced The reward system has been interrupted. Addiction and alcoholism is based on a reward system. After using the substance the person is rewarded by getting high. When the reward is taken away, the person stops using. This system is based on operant conditioning.

B.   Desiparamine- takes away the craving for cocaine by relieving the depression. One that is actively using cocaine continues to use cocaine even though there are numerous consequences. The reason for this is that cocaine makes one very high. When the high is over the person becomes very depressed. The major component of cocaine withdrawal is depression. Desiparamine is used to treat the depression. The depression is what causes the cravings. By diminishing the depression, the cravings are also diminished. Hence the need to use massive amounts on the drug cocaine also diminishes very much in a very decisive way. Addiction can be treated through pharmacology.

C.   Antabuse is another pharmacological way in which to treat addiction. Another name for Antabuse is disuffiam. Antabuse works by making a person violently ill when they ingest alcohol. The person soon learns not to use alcohol in order to avoid the awful effects of alcohol use. When a person drinks alcohol after taking antabuse, they begin to throw-up and shake violently. The disadvantage of this is that a person who is planning on drinking will stop taking the antabuse for a period of time to allow the antabuse   to get out of their system. When they feel that the antabuse is out of their system, they will usually get drunk. This is because the antabuse doesn't treat the abnormal mental cognition patterns that have allowed the person to consistently get drunk over a period of time. These mental cognitions have to be changed or the person will continue to get drunk. Antabuse with therapy should prove to be effective for treating alcohol.

D.   Methadone is used in the treatment of heroin addiction. Methadone only seems to prolong the heroin addiction rather than treat it. Methadone is used as maintenance. The feeling by the overall general society is that it is better to have the person hooked on methadone rather than have the person breaking the law and being a menace to society trying to get the money to use heroin. Many heroin addicts will get on methadone because it is a free high. They are not usually willing to pay the price or go through the pain of withdrawal in order to get off the devastating and dehumanizing drug heroin. Once a person becomes addicted to methadone, it is very difficult to get off the drug. Many addicts say that their "bones" ache when they try to detox from methadone. According to many addicts "being addicted to methadone is a living hell.

E. Anti-Depressants- are used in the treatment of cocaine addiction. It is felt that many cocaine addicts are really depressed individuals that are self-medicating themselves by using cocaine. Depression may be caused by a number of factors, acting alone or in combination. The tendency to become depressed is inherited- it runs in families. The same is true for high blood pressure, diabetes, and other illnesses. Depression often makes people become less interested in their usual activities. They find it difficult to care about things that used to be important. They have to push to get things done. Even little things may seem burdensome. Many people who have depression say that they are bored, or, even if they have no sleep problems, that they are tired all the time or sluggish. A reduced interest in sex is also common. People with depression often feel negatively about themselves, the world around them, and the future. They may feel guilty abut things in the past. many people with depression feel that they are worthless or that their depression is a punishment for something they have done or left undone. Depression can lead to feelings of insecurity and the need to be dependent on others. It can also lead to poor grooming and personal hygiene.

Depression makes it hard to think clearly, and decisions about even small things may be difficult to make. Often, people who have depression cannot concentrate easily-so work and daily routines become less efficient, and feelings of failure and disgust may appear. Many depressed people think about death. Thoughts-and actions-related to death may occur as part of a wish to end pain, suffering and confusion. As with many medical illnesses, depression causes a number of symptoms. The symptoms can interfere with your ability to perform or enjoy your usual daily activities. In fact, many days of work are missed each year by people who are unable to function because of depression. And, over the course of the illness, the particular symptoms someone feels can change, and the severity of the symptoms can also change. Depressed mood and even crying spells are symptoms of depression. Many people who have depression. Many people who have depression, however, are not sad at all or may have difficulty putting into words the way they fee.

Depression can start at any age, but most first episodes occur in the mid 20's to the mid 30's. Many people who have depression are never diagnosed, and the first episode in particular may be missed or left untreated. The symptoms of the illness develop gradually over days or weeks. most untreated episodes last from 6 to 24 months, but for as many as 1 in 10, people the episode may last longer.

Most people with depression recover from the illness. They find that their symptoms go away completely and that they are then able to function as well as they could before the episode. But recovery from an episode may not be complete-some symptoms may remain even though they may become less intense. More than half of the people who have one episode of depression will have another. Many people remain symptom free for years before having another episode. Other people have more frequent episodes and find that the frequency increases with age. And some people have continuing, chronic problems with depression. Therefore they are using cocaine to treat their depression unknowingly. This is one reason why anti-depressants have been very useful in treating cocaine addiction. Another reason that anti-depressants have been effective in treating cocaine addiction, is that it is very hard for a person that is hooked on cocaine to get past the withdrawal stage of cocaine. Cocaine is the most addictive drug that there is. What makes cocaine so addictive is the very deep depression that a person goes though when they stop using cocaine. The depression that accompanies the withdrawal from cocaine is so bad that many people have killed themselves. An example is Carrol O'Connor's son committed suicide. Therefore many people continue using and stay addicted, spending massive amounts of money to keep their habit going in order to avoid facing the withdrawals and depression that comes when a person stops using cocaine. In fact, it is felt by many addictionologist, that many of the overdoses from cocaine are brought about by cocaine addicts using massive amounts of cocaine in order to get out of very deep depressions.

With respect to its broader scientific application, metabolism, which has long been studied, is emerging with new implications for the study of alcoholism and its medical consequences. For instance, how is metabolism related to the resistance of some individuals to alcoholism? We know that some inherited abnormalities in metabolism (e.g., flushing reaction among some persons of Asian descent) promote resistance to alcoholism. Recent data from two large-scale NIAAA-supported genetics studies suggest that alcohol dehydrogenase genes may be associated with differential resistance and vulnerability to alcohol. These findings are important to the study of why some people develop alcoholism and others do not. Studies of metabolism also can identify alternate paths of alcohol metabolism, which may help explain how alcohol speeds up the elimination of some substances (e.g., barbiturates) and increases the toxicity of others (e.g., acetaminophen). This information will help health care providers in advising patients on alcohol-drug interactions that may decrease the effectiveness of some therapeutic medications or render others harmful.

It is a fact. The manner in which some individuals metabolize alcohol in many cases determines whether or not these people will become addicted to alcohol. Many individuals are able to drink massive amounts of alcohol without even getting a little disoriented. While others are able to get dysphoric with just minute amounts of alcohol.

This many researchers believe is the primary reason that many people become alcoholic while others do not. Yes, how one's body metabolizes the alcohol is a major factor that determines whether or not a person will become alcoholic.

Even though we do not understand fully the biochemical mechanisms of immunity and susceptibility, we have a fair amount of data that identify certain populations as high risk alcoholism if they drink. No child is doomed by heredity to be an alcoholic, but we know that statistically the children of alcoholic ancestry are much more vulnerable. We must also mention truants, school dropouts, and native American Youth, among others. Liver enzyme tests or EEG may eventually enable us to identify those more likely to develop alcoholism, who would then be educated as to the nature of the illness without using scare tactics. To say that we live in a drinking society describes only a part of the reality. Social pressures to drink, and sometimes overwhelmingly takes over. The BudLight advertising budget is twenty-five times that of the NIAAA prevention and education budget, and the alcoholic beverage industry in the United States spends about $2 billion or $5.48 million a day on advertising, those businessmen presumably get what they pay for: $2 billion worth of pressure on us to drink (a billion in television and another in print media. They claim that they are not after consumption but only at a choice of brands, yet the net effect cannot help but promote drinking rather than abstinence. (Actually, the ads are aimed at adding new drinkers and at heavy drinkers; if everybody practiced moderation as they pretend to advocate, the alcoholic beverage industry would lose nearly half its business.) One issue of Ms. magazine contained twice as many ads for liquor as for cosmetics. College newspapers in 1986 ad thirty-four times as much space in ads for beer as for books. The atmosphere this creates is bolstered by the attractive cocktail waitress who appeals to your machismo with the subtle implication that you are not much of a man if you don't order up; by the modeling of parents who make hospitality synonymous with offering a drink; by the portrayal of alcohol drinking on television shows out of all proportion to the actual rate as compared with nonalcoholic beverage use; by our tolerance and even admiration of excessive drinking; and by slogans and customs that make the nondrinker feel unsophisticated and antisocial.

Conclusion: Consequences:

Drug use behavior can cause many negative health-related consequences, including fatal and nonfatal overdose, infection, and AIDS (acquired immunodeficiency syndrome) and other sexually transmitted diseases. Drug use also may increase the risk of accidents and injuries, complications of pregnancy, adverse birth outcomes such as low birth weight an birth defects, and suicide and other psychiatric problems.

The claims of association between drug use and many of these negative consequences are based primarily on case studies or case reports. Few known methodologically sound, epidemiologic case-control or prospective studies have been done in either white or nonwhite populations. What is known to date, however, suggests that minority populations may be overrepresented among those who suffer form the adverse consequences of drug abuse. The Department of Health and Human Services Task Force on African American and Minority Health found that among African Americans, mortality rates for chronic disease and cirrhosis were nearly twice as high as the rates among whites and that in the 2000's, cocaine-related deaths among African an Americans tripled while only doubling among whites . The status of American Indians and Alaska Natives is reported to be below that of other Americans in many epidemiologic reports. In 2003-04 death rates for American Indians under age 45 substantially exceeded those for whites of the same age. Most striking is the finding that while African Americans and Hispanics together comprise about 21 percent of the U.S. population, they account for about 50 percent of the reported cases of AIDS. African American in particular are overrepresented among total AIDS cases. Twice as many AIDS cases involve African American females as white and Hispanic females. Similarly, while African American males account for approximately 12 percent of the total male population, they represent nearly 30 percent of AIDS cases among men. The number of Hispanics with AIDS also is sizable. Nearly 17 percent of AIDS cases among males and 20 percent of AIDS among females cases involve Hispanics. Injecting drug use is the exposure category for a large proportion of the group that has contracted AIDS. Injecting drug use is the primary mode of transmission for HIV infection in heterosexual and pediatric AIDS cases. In the United States, 109,393 of the 435,317 (25 percent) AIDS cases reported through December 1994 (among persons ages 13 and older) have resulted directly from injecting drugs. additional 28,521 cases were attributed to men who have sex with men and inject drugs. Among women with AIDS, as of December 1994 the largest proportion of cases were contracted through injecting drugs for whites (43 percent), African American (50 percent), Hispanics (46 percent), American Indians and Alaska Native (50 percent).

DRUG-RELATED EMERGENCY ROOM EPISODES

Drug-related hospital ER cases provide one measure of the health risks associated with drug use. Over time they indicate increases or decreases in the incidence of problems associated with a particular drug. These trends may be influenced by a number of factors including changes in prevalence of use, dosages, potency, frequency of use, aging of existing users, routes of administration, the combined use of two or more drugs. and the access to care.

DRUG-RELATED DEATHS

Medical examiner data presented in DAWN reports are collected from a nonrandom sample and are not statistically representative of the Nation or of the respective metropolitan area. A drug death is defined as any death in which drug use is a contributory factor but not necessarily the sole cause; consequently, causation of death by the drug is not implied.

Some medical examiners may include cases involving circumstantial evidence and other medical examiners may report only drug-related deaths confirmed through toxicological analyses. In light of these limitations, caution should be used in interpreting these data, The top three drugs (i.e., those mentioned most frequently) reported for decedents by medical examiners across all sex and racial/ethnic groups were cocaine, heroin/morphine, and alcohol-in-combination.

Both African American and Hispanic decedents were more likely than whites to have used cocaine whereas white decedents were more likely than African Americans and Hispanics to have used diazepam or methamphetamine/speed. Hispanics have the highest percentage of accidental drug related deaths (80.5 percent), followed by African Americans (62.9 percent) and compared with the relatively low percentages of drug related suicides among Hispanics (11.1 percent) and African Americans (7.8 percent).

RESIDUAL EFFECTS OF ALCOHOL-

Alcohol intoxication refers to the varied behavioral, neurological, and psychological sequelae of alcohol ingesting. The average-sized individual metabolizes between 7 and 10 grams of alcohol per hour, which corresponds to approximately 1 ounce of 90-proof spirits or 12 ounces of beer. As the amount of alcohol ingested exceeds metabolic capacity, the level of alcohol in the blood increases. For the individual who has not developed a high degree of tolerance to alcohol, i.e., the social drinker, the degree of intoxication and the observed impairment correspond roughly to measured blood alcohol level (BAL: milligrams of alcohol per 100 ml of blood, or mg percent).

After one or two drinks, the non-tolerant individual experiences only minor changes in coordination, behavior, or mood. However, as BAL increases above 100mg percent (approximately five drinks in 1 hour for a 160-pound man, most social drinkers begin to demonstrate significant sighs of intoxication, including impaired speech, ataxia, mood lability, impaired judgment, and memory and attention deficits. At dosage levels exceeding 200mg percent, these symptoms intensify. Marked dysarthria and ataxia are accompanied by extensive impairment of judgment, psychomotor skills, attention and memory, and mood control. At dosage levels exceeding 300mg of alcohol per 100ml of blood, the anesthetic action of alcohol predominates, with the possibility of coma, respiratory failure, and death increasing dramatically at BALs between 400 and 700mg percent. Although virtually all alcoholics experience eat least some of the generally benign symptoms of withdrawal, only 5 percent of alcoholics hospitalized for major withdrawal experience alcohol withdrawal delirium. Peak incidence of the disorder is between the ages of 30 and 50 with a decline in frequency after the age of 60. Improvements in the effective hospital management of the syndrome have resulted in a significant drop in mortality rates, with estimates ranging between 5 percent and 50 percent. Men are at a higher risk to develop the disorder than women, probable because of both the higher incidence of alcoholism in men and differences in drinking patterns between men and women. This disorder is the result of chronic alcohol abuse. AMNESTIC DISORDERS:

Korsakoff first described the unique amnestic syndrome, which would subsequently bear his name, in 1887. In its acute phase, the syndrome is characterized by mental confusion and disorientation to time, place, or person; in its chronic stages, the confusional state subsides, and patients again become alert-but typically apathetic and lacking in spontaneity or self-direction. As indicated above, the memory function is severely disturbed: there is a marked deterioration in short-term memory, coupled with varying degrees of retrograde amnesia. Confabulation is also frequently associated with Korsakoff's syndrome. However, the presence of confabulation is not required for the diagnosis.

With respect to its broader scientific application, metabolism, which has long been studied, is emerging with new implications for the study of alcoholism and its medical consequences. For instance, how is metabolism related to the resistance of some individuals to alcoholism? We know that some inherited abnormalities in metabolism (e.g., flushing reaction among some persons of Asian descent) promote resistance to alcoholism. Recent data from two large-scale NIAAA-supported genetics studies suggest that alcohol dehydrogenase genes may be associated with differential resistance and vulnerability to alcohol. These findings are important to the study of why some people develop alcoholism and others do not. Studies of metabolism also can identify alternate paths of alcohol metabolism, which may help explain how alcohol speeds up the elimination of some substances (e.g., barbiturates) and increases the toxicity of others (e.g., acetaminophen). This information will help health care providers in advising patients on alcohol-drug interactions that may decrease the effectiveness of some therapeutic medications or render others harmful.

It is a fact. The manner in which some individuals metabolize alcohol in many cases determines whether or not these people will become addicted to alcohol. Many individuals are able to drink massive amounts of alcohol without even getting a little disoriented. While others are able to get dysphoric with just minute amounts of alcohol. This many researchers believe is the primary reason that many people become alcoholic while others do not. Yes, how one's body metabolizes the alcohol is a major factor that determines whether or not a person will become alcoholic.

Even though we do not understand fully the biochemical mechanisms of immunity and susceptibility, we have a fair amount of data that identify certain populations as high risk alcoholism if they drink. No child is doomed by heredity to be an alcoholic, but we know that statistically the children of alcoholic ancestry are much more vulnerable. We must also mention truants, school dropouts, and native American Youth, among others. Liver enzyme tests or EEG may eventually enable us to identify those more likely to develop alcoholism, who would then be educated as to the nature of the illness without using scare tactics.

To say that we live in a drinking society describes only a part of the reality. Social pressures to drink, and drinking profusely is encouraged. The Bud Light ad dr advertising budget is twenty-five times that of the **NIAAA** prevention and education budget, and the alcoholic beverage industry in the United States spends about $2 billion or $5.48 million a day on advertising, those businessmen presumably get what they pay for: $2 billion worth of pressure on us to drink (a billion in television and another in print media;,. They claim that they are not after consumption but only at a choice of brands, yet the net effect cannot help but promote drinking rather than. Alcoholism is a chronic disease that makes your body dependent on alcohol. You may be obsessed with alcohol and unable to control how much you drink, even though your drinking is causing serious problems with your relationships, health, work and finances. It's possible to have a problem with alcohol, but not display all the characteristics of alcoholism. This is known as "alcohol abuse," which means you engage in excessive drinking that causes health or social problems, but you aren't dependent on alcohol and haven't fully lost control over the use of alcohol.

Although many people assume otherwise, alcoholism is a treatable disease. Medications, counseling and self-help groups are among the therapies that can provide ongoing support to help you recover from alcohol. Yes, alcoholism is a disease. The craving that an alcoholic feels for alcohol can be as strong as the need for food or water.

An alcoholic will continue to drink despite serious family, health, or legal problems.

Like many other diseases, alcoholism is chronic, meaning that it lasts a person's lifetime; it usually follows a predictable course; and it has symptoms. The risk for developing alcoholism is influenced both by a person's genes and by his or her lifestyle.

Is alcoholism inherited?

Research shows that the risk for developing alcoholism does indeed run in families. The genes a person inherits partially explain this pattern, but lifestyle is also a factor. Currently, researchers are working to discover the actual genes that put people at risk for alcoholism. Your friends, the amount of <u>stress</u> in your life, and how readily available alcohol is also are factors that may increase your risk for alcoholism. But remember: Risk is not destiny. Just because alcoholism tends to run in families doesn't mean that a child of an alcoholic parent will automatically become an alcoholic too. Some people develop alcoholism even though no one in their family has a drinking problem. By the same token, not all children of alcoholic families get into trouble with alcohol. Knowing you are at risk is important, though, because then you can take steps to protect yourself from developing problems with alcohol.

Can alcoholism be cured?

No, alcoholism cannot be cured at this time. Even if an alcoholic hasn't been drinking for a long time, he or she can still suffer a <u>relapse</u>. Not drinking is the safest course for most people with alcoholism.

Can alcoholism be treated?

Yes, alcoholism can be treated. Alcoholism treatment programs use both counseling and medications to help a person stop drinking. Treatment has helped many people stop drinking and rebuild their lives.

Alcohol Dependence is a condition characterized by the harmful consequences of repeated alcohol use, a pattern of compulsive alcohol use, and (sometimes) physiological dependence on alcohol (i.e., tolerance and/or symptoms of withdrawal). This disorder is only diagnosed when these behaviors become persistent and very disabling or distressing.

Complications:

School and job performance may suffer either from hangovers or from actual intoxication on the job or at school; child care or household responsibilities may be neglected; and alcohol-related absences may occur from school or job. The individual may use alcohol in physically hazardous circumstances (e.g., drunk driving or operating machinery while intoxicated). Legal difficulties may arise because of alcohol use (e.g., arrests for intoxicated behavior or for drunk driving). Individuals with this disorder may continue to abuse alcohol despite the knowledge that continued drinking poses significant social or interpersonal problems for them (e.g., violent arguments with spouse while intoxicated, child abuse). Alcohol intoxication causes significant intellectual impairment (and stupid behavior). Once a pattern of compulsive use develops, individuals with this disorder may devote substantial periods of time to obtaining and consuming alcoholic beverages. These individuals continue to use alcohol despite evidence of adverse psychological or physical consequences (e.g., depression, blackouts, liver disease, or other complications). Individuals with this disorder are at increased risk for accidents, violence, and suicide. It is estimated that 1 in 5 intensive care unit admissions in some urban hospitals is related to alcohol and that 40% of people in U.S.A. experience an alcohol-related accident at some time in their lives, with alcohol accounting for up to 55% of fatal driving events. More than one-half of all murderers and their victims are believed to have been intoxicated with alcohol at the time of the murder. Severe Alcohol Intoxication also contributes to disinhibition and feelings of sadness and irritability, which contribute to suicide attempts and completed suicides.

Only 5% of individuals with Alcohol Dependence ever experience severe complications of withdrawal (e.g., delirium, grand mal seizures). However, repeated intake of high doses of alcohol can affect nearly every organ system, especially the gastrointestinal tract, cardiovascular system, and the central and peripheral nervous system. Gastrointestinal effects include gastritis, stomach or duodenal ulcers, and, in about 15% of those who use alcohol heavily, liver cirrhosis and pancreatitis. There is also an increased rate of cancer of the esophagus, stomach, and other parts of the gastrointestinal tract. One of the most common associated general medical conditions is low-grade hypertension. There is an elevated risk of heart disease. Peripheral neuropathy may be evidenced by muscular weakness, paresthesias, and decreased peripheral sensation. Most persistent central nervous system effects include cognitive deficits, severe memory impairment, and degenerative changes in the cerebellum (leading to poor balance and coordination). One devastating central nervous system effect is the relatively rare Alcohol-Induced Persisting Amnestic Disorder (Wernicke-Korsakoff syndrome) better known as wet brain, in which there is a dramatic impairment in short-term memory. Men may develop erectile dysfunction and decreased testosterone levels. Repeated heavy drinking in women is associated with menstrual irregularities and, during pregnancy, with spontaneous abortion and fetal alcohol syndrome (leading to mentally retarded, hyperactive children). Alcohol Dependence can suppress immune mechanisms and predispose individuals to infections (e.g., pneumonia) and increase the risk for cancer.

Comorbidity:

Individuals with Alcohol Dependence are at increased risk for Major Depressive Disorder, other Substance-Related Disorders (e.g., drug addiction), Conduct Disorder in adolescents, Antisocial and Emotionally Unstable (Borderline) Personality Disorders, Schizophrenia, and Bipolar Disorder.

Prevalence:

Alcohol use is highly prevalent in most Western countries. However, in most Asian cultures, the overall prevalence of Alcohol-Related Disorders is relatively low. In Muslim countries, the Islamic religion strictly prohibits alcohol (hence the rates of Alcohol-Related Disorders are very low). In the Western countries, this disorder occurs much more commonly in males (with a male-to-female ratio of 5:1). The lifetime risk of Alcohol Dependence is approximately 15% in the general population. In any year, 5% of the general population will actively be suffering from Alcohol Dependence.

Alcohol Dependence has a variable course that is frequently characterized by periods of remission and relapse. The first episode of Alcohol Intoxication is likely to occur in the mid-teens, with the age at onset of Alcohol Dependence peaking in the 20s to mid-30s. The large majority of those who develop Alcohol Dependency do so by their late 30s.

Familial Pattern:

Alcohol Dependence often has a familial pattern, and it is estimated that 40%-60% of the variance of risk is explained by genetic influences. The risk for Alcohol Dependence is 3 to 4 times higher in close relatives of people with Alcohol Dependence. Most studies have found a significantly higher risk for Alcohol Dependence in the monozygotic twin than in the dizygotic twin of a person with Alcohol Dependence. Adoption studies have revealed a 3- to 4-fold increase in risk for Alcohol Dependence in the children of individuals with Alcohol Dependence when these children were adopted away at birth and raised by adoptive parents who did not have this disorder.

Treatment:

Follow-up studies of the typical person with an Alcohol Use Disorder show a higher than 65% 1-year abstinence rate following treatment. Even among less functional and homeless individuals with Alcohol Dependence who complete a treatment program, as many as 60% are abstinent at 3 months, and 45% at 1 year. Some individuals (perhaps 20% or more) with Alcohol Dependence achieve long-term sobriety even without treatment.

Alcoholism is a condition resulting from excessive drinking of and dependence on beverages that contain alcohol. Alcoholism, also known as alcohol dependence, is a disease with physical, psychological, and social health issues. Those affected experience:

Physical dependence--withdrawal symptoms, such as nausea, sweating, shakiness, and anxiety after stopping drinking

Tolerance--the need to drink greater amounts of alcohol to get "high"

Craving--a strong need, or urge, to drink

*Loss of control--*Not being able to stop drinking once drinking has begun

According to the <u>National Institute on Alcohol Abuse and Alcoholism (NIAAA)</u>, nearly 20% of patients treated in general medical practices report drinking at levels considered "risky" or "hazardous." They may be at risk for developing alcohol-related problems as a result.

The NIAAA defines risky drinking by both daily and weekly consumption of "standard drinks," with one standard drink equal to about 12 ounces of beer, 5 ounces of wine, or 1.5 ounces of hard liquor. For men, 5 or more drinks a day or 15 or more a week is considered risky, while for women it is 4 or more a day or 8 or more a week. People's response to alcohol is individual, however, and may be affected by their size, age, general state of health, and by the medications they are taking. In some, fewer drinks can still cause health problems. Since there is no known "safe" alcohol level for pregnant women, the Surgeon General advises women who are, or are planning to be, pregnant to abstain from drinking.

The major health risks of alcoholism include <u>liver disease</u>, <u>heart disease</u>, certain forms of cancer, <u>pancreatitis</u>, and nervous system disorders. These conditions often develop gradually and may become evident only after long-term heavy drinking. The liver is particularly vulnerable to diseases related to heavy drinking, most commonly, alcoholic hepatitis (inflammation) or <u>cirrhosis</u> (scarring of the liver). Women tend to be more sensitive to the effects of alcohol and may develop alcohol-related health problems sooner and after consuming less alcohol than men do. Alcohol use in pregnant women can lead to miscarriages, and to the malformation of organs (such as the brain and heart) in their unborn children. According to the March of Dimes, up to 40,000 babies a year are born with some degree of damage related to alcohol.

Experts have defined a second problem, called alcohol abuse, as something different from alcoholism. The difference is that those who abuse alcohol do not have an extremely strong craving for alcohol, loss of control over drinking, or physical dependence. People who abuse alcohol also can develop the physical symptoms related to alcoholism, however, and suffer from its effects. Alcohol abuse is defined as a pattern of drinking that results in particular situations, such as failure to fulfill major work, school or home duties, or having recurring alcohol-related legal problems, such as arrests for driving under the influence of alcohol.

Alcoholism is a chronic, often progressive disease in which a person craves alcohol and drinks despite repeated alcohol-related problems (like losing a job or a relationship). Alcoholism involves a physical dependence on alcohol, but other factors include genetic, psychological, and cultural influences.

Becoming addicted to alcohol is a gradual process that happens as alcohol changes the level of chemicals in your brain, especially gamma-amino butyric acid or GABA (which stops you from being impulsive) and dopamine (which is linked with pleasurable feelings). As the levels of these chemicals change, you crave alcohol to make yourself feel good again.

About 18 million people in the United States abuse alcohol, and estimates suggest that more than 70 million Americans have dealt with alcoholism in their family. Alcohol is involved in almost half or all traffic deaths in the U.S.

Alcoholism is characterized by craving for alcohol and a loss of control over drinking, along with a physical dependence (meaning that the person experiences withdrawal symptoms when not drinking) and a tolerance for alcohol (meaning the person needs to drink greater amounts to feel "good"). Before entering recovery, most alcoholics will deny they have a problem. People who abuse alcohol but are not dependent on it may have similar symptoms, but they don't feel the same craving to drink and usually don't experience withdrawal symptoms.

Signs and Symptoms:

- Drinking by yourself or in secret
- Craving alcohol
- Not being able to control the amount you drink
- Blackouts (not remembering events or conversations)
- Becoming irritable when you can't get a drink at your regular time
- Having legal problems or an inability to sustain a relationship or a job
- Withdrawal symptoms, such as nausea, sweating, shakiness, and anxiety, when you stop drinking
- Needing more alcohol to feel its effects
- Liver disease

Risk Factors:

If you have a family history of alcohol abuse, you are more likely to develop the condition than someone without a family history. Other factors that may increase your risk include:

- Beginning to drink early, by age 16 or sooner
- Drinking more than one to two drinks per day
- Smoking cigarettes (particularly teenagers)
- Being under a lot of stress
- Having a preexisting psychiatric disorder (such as depression or anxiety)

Diagnosis:

If you or someone you care for is experiencing symptoms associated with alcoholism, you should see your doctor. He or she can help make a diagnosis and guide you in determining which treatment or combination of therapies will work best. You should know that, because most alcoholics deny they have a problem, they are often unlikely to seek treatment by themselves. Friends and family members may have to convince them to seek help.

- Your doctor will take a history and do a physical exam. Questions that he or she may ask include:

- Have you ever thought that you needed to cut back on the amount of alcohol you drink?

- Has a spouse, friend or coworker ever annoyed you by asking you to drink less?

- Do you ever feel guilty about the amount that you drink?

- Do you ever drink in the morning or early in the day to soothe a hangover, get the day started, or get rid of the shakes?

- Blood tests generally aren't helpful because they only show recent alcohol consumption. But your doctor may order liver function tests to see if there has been damage to your liver from alcohol..

Preventive Care:

If you drink, do so only in moderation — no more than two drinks per day if you are a man and no more than one drink per day if you are a woman.

Early intervention is key, especially with teenagers. To prevent teen drinking, consider the following:

- Stay involved and interested in your teenager's life.

- Talk openly to your children, especially pre-teens and teens, about the widespread presence and dangers of alcohol and drugs.

- Have clear, non-negotiable rules about not using alcohol and drugs.

- Act as a role model – don't drink excessively, use other drugs, or smoke.

- Strongly urge your children to not smoke.

- Encourage your children to become active in sports, music, the arts, or other activities.

- Know where your children and teens are at all times and make sure that there is always adult supervision.

- Monitor your teenager for aggressive behavior, feelings of anger or depression, and poor school performance. If any of these develop, consider whether alcohol may be a reason.

- Never drink and drive or allow your teenager to be driven in the car by someone who has been drinking.

Treatment Approach:

The first and most important step in getting treatment for alcoholism is recognizing that you have a problem. Often, family members and close friends may urge treatment for the person with the addiction.

Treatment and ongoing recovery must address both physical and psychological addiction and may include inpatient treatment and/or Alcoholics Anonymous (AA). In an inpatient or residential program, the person generally stays in a hospital or center for 28 days, undergoing first detoxification (usually four to seven days) and then individual and group therapy emphasizing abstinence. Talk to a doctor about what is best for you or your loved one.

Lifestyle

- Attend Alcoholics Anonymous.
- Family members should attend Al-Anon to learn how to help the person with the addiction and to get help and support themselves.
- Exercise regularly to help reduce cravings.

Medications

Your provider may prescribe the following medications.

For alcohol withdrawal

Benzodiazepines — tranquilizers used during the first few days of treatment to help you withdraw safely from alcohol. These drugs include

- Diazepam (Valium)
- Chlordiazepoxid (Librium)
- Lorazepam (Ativan)
- Oxazepam (Serax)

Anticonvulsants — may also help with withdrawal symptoms and don't have the potential for abuse (as benzodiazepines do). They include

- Carbamazepine (Tegretol)
- Valprioc acid (Depakote)
- Phenytoin (Dilantin)

Drinking alcohol is woven into the social fabric of our culture, and indeed many people enjoy the social and cultural connection of sharing a drink together. However, because drinking is so common in our society, realizing you or a loved one has a drinking problem can be a challenge. The consequences of alcohol abuse are serious. Alcohol abuse causes extensive damage to your health, your loved ones, and society. It results in thousands of innocent deaths each year, and exacerbates situations involving violent crimes and domestic violence. Learn about alcoholism signs and symptoms, what you can do, and how you can help a loved one.

Social drinking is common and popular is many cultures all over the world. In several cultures, for example, a glass of wine or beer with a meal is common practice. Celebrations are often punctuated with a glass of champagne or other celebratory cocktail. And in many jobs, going out for drinks after work or entertaining clients with alcohol is the norm.

The difference between social drinking and *alcohol abuse* is when alcohol becomes your focus. You might only want to attend social events that involve alcohol, or you can't enjoy yourself. Getting to the bar, or making a drink after coming home from work becomes more important than connecting with friends or family. Alcohol might be your way to avoid painful feelings or troubled relationships. And you might resort to dangerous behavior, like driving while drunk or even increased violent behavior. Increased dependence on alcohol leads to *alcoholism, where you are physically dependant on alcohol and have lost control of the amount you drink.*

Myths about alcohol abuse

Myth: Alcoholics have no will power. If they were stronger they could just stop drinking.

Fact: Alcoholism affects brain chemistry, which causes you to feel compelled to drink alcohol. Usually you can only stop drinking if you receive continuing help and treatment.

Myth: I can't have a drinking problem. I have control over it because I only drink on the weekends.

Fact: When you abstain from drinking for a certain period of time and then consume a large quantity of alcohol in a very small span of time, this is called binge drinking. It is a common symptom of alcohol abuse.

Myth: Drinking is not a "real" addiction like drug abuse.

Fact: Alcohol *is* a drug, and alcohol abuse is every bit as real as drug abuse. Alcohol addiction has serious long term health and legal consequences, and withdrawal can be deadly.

Causes of alcohol abuse

Why can one person drink responsibly, while another drinks to the point of losing their health, their family and their job? There is no one simple reason. Alcohol abuse and addiction is due to many factors. What's more, since drinking is so common in our society, problem drinking can be hard to identify. Do you drink to share enjoyment or share a connection with others? If drinking is the *only* way you feel comfortable connecting to others, or you drink to mask depression, grief, anxiety or loneliness, you are at risk for alcohol abuse. Some other risk factors include:

- **Family history of alcoholism.** While the interplay between genetics and environment is not entirely clear, if you have a family history of addiction, you are at higher risk for abusing alcohol.

- **History of mental illness.** Alcohol abuse can worsen mental illness or even create new symptoms.

- **Peer pressure.** If people around you drink heavily, it's hard to resist. If you are a teenager, you might feel you won't be accepted. If drinking is common practice for work celebrations or entertaining clients, you might feel pressure to conform.

  Stressful situations or a big life change. If you have a major change or a stressful situation in your life, without other coping skills, you might turn to alcohol to help you get through.

Signs & symptoms of alcoholism

How can I tell if I or a loved one has problems with drinking?

Although different people may use alcohol at different levels, the basic pattern is the same. Drinking becomes more and more important than anything else, including job, friends and family. Alcohol starts to increasingly affect you physically and emotionally, often impairing judgment to a dangerous level.

How serious is the drinking problem?

Alcohol abusers, or problem drinkers, are people who drink too much on a regular basis. The alcohol use is self-destructive or can present a danger to others, but they still demonstrate some ability to set limits and establish some measure of control over their drinking. While some people are able to maintain this pattern for a long amount of time, alcohol abusers are at risk for progressing to *alcoholism*. This might happen in response to a large stressful event, such as retirement or losing a job. Or it might gradually progress as tolerance to alcohol increases.

When alcohol abuse progresses to **alcoholism***, also called* **alcohol addiction** *or* **alcohol dependence***,* alcohol becomes essential to function. Alcoholic symptoms include a physical dependence on alcohol, and inability to stop despite severe physical and psychological consequences. Some alcoholics can hold down a job or appear to be functioning on the surface, but the drinking inevitably leads to impaired job performance and troubled relationships.

The National Institute on Alcohol Abuse and Alcoholism provides a screening questionnaire for assessing the differences between alcohol abuse and alcoholic dependence. Remember, though, the bottom line is how alcohol affects you. If it is affecting your relationships, job, or health, yet you can't seem to stop yourself, then the problem is serious. This is alcoholism according to latest definitions of alcoholism.

Physical signs of alcohol abuse and alcoholism

- While intoxicated: slurred speech, dizziness, clumsiness or unsteadiness
- Blackouts, when you drink so much you pass out
- Weight loss

- Unexplained sore or upset stomach
- Redness in the face or cheeks
- Numbness or tingling in hands and feet

Tolerance and withdrawal symptoms

The more alcohol you drink, the more your body depends on it. You need more and more alcohol to have the same effect, called *tolerance*. If you drink heavily, you will have *withdrawal symptoms* if you stop drinking. Do you need a drink to steady the shakes in the morning? You've built up a tolerance for alcohol. Other withdrawal symptoms include sweating, shaking, nausea and vomiting, confusion, and in severe cases seizures and hallucinations. These symptoms can be medically dangerous. Talk to a medical professional if you are a heavy drinker and want to quit.

Mental signs of alcohol abuse and alcoholism

- Unable to control drinking: "just one drink" rapidly leads to more
- Drinking leads to dangerous situations like driving drunk, walking in an unsafe area
- Increased irritability, agitation and anger, lowered threshold for violence
- Avoiding activities that do not involve the opportunity to drink
- Excessive weeping and emotional displays
- Unexplained absences and sick days from work, or difficulty making commitments
- Oversleeping or difficulty sleeping

Alcohol abuse in special populations

- **Teenagers.** Teenagers notoriously like their privacy, are often irritable and cranky, and like to sleep in. How can you tell if your teen has an alcohol problem? Look for marked changes in behavior, appearance and health. Is your teen suddenly having trouble in school? Does he or she seem more and more isolated, or have a new group of friends? Your teen might have an unusually hard time getting up or appear sick regularly in the morning. If you have alcohol in the home, do the levels decrease faster than they should? Is the alcohol watered down?

- **Older adults**. Alcohol abuse is challenging to detect in older adults. Increased alcohol use might happen as an older adult retires, loses a loved one, or has to move. Older adults are more sensitive to the effects of alcohol as their metabolism changes. Since older adults often do much of their drinking at home, problems functioning often go undetected. Clumsiness, unsteadiness or confusion might be attributed to the natural aging process.

Effects of alcohol abuse

What makes alcohol problems so challenging to face? Similar to drug abuse, alcohol abuse doesn't only affect the health, finances and stability of the person drinking. It reaches family, friends, colleagues-- and even the community. What's more, the strong denial and rationalization of the person using alcohol makes it extremely difficult to get help, and can make concerned family members feel like they are the problem.

Health effects of alcohol abuse

Long-term alcohol use can cause serious health complications, affecting virtually every organ in your body. These effects include:

- Liver inflammation, which can lead to cirrhosis, a serious, irreversible liver condition

- Increased risk of heart disease, stroke and cancer

- Stomach problems and nutritional deficiencies

- Neurological problems such as confusion, numbness and trouble with memory

- Birth defects

- Erectile dysfunction

Staying addicted: denial and rationalization

One of the most powerful effects of alcohol abuse and addiction is denial. The urge to drink is so strong that the mind finds many ways to rationalize more drinking. Someone abusing alcohol may drastically underestimate how much they are drinking, how much it is costing them, and how much time it takes away from their family and work. Denial is so powerful that an alcoholic often sincerely believes that there is no problem. They may lash out at concerned family members, so convincingly that family members might feel like they are exaggerating and overstating the problem.

This denial and rationalization can lead to increased problems with work, finances and relationships. The person abusing alcohol may blame an "unfair boss' for losing her job, or a 'nagging wife' for why he is increasingly going out with friends to the bar. While work and relationship stresses happen to everyone, an overall pattern of deterioration and blaming others may be a sign of trouble.

Effects of alcohol abuse on the family

Sadly, alcohol abuse and addiction doesn't only affect the person abusing alcohol. It affects friends, family and the entire society. Child abuse and neglect is much more common when there is alcohol abuse in the family. The abuser may neglect a child's basic needs due to drinking. Lack of impulse control can lead to increased physical and emotional abuse. Alcohol abuse by a pregnant woman affects the developing baby's health. Domestic violence also happens more frequently. Abusing alcohol leads to higher risk of injuries and death to self and others in car accidents.

Family stress

If you have someone you love who drinks too much, it is an enormous emotional strain. You might feel obligated to cover for the alcoholic, cutting back from work to deal with the problems that come up from the drinking— or working more to make financial ends meet. You might not be able to see friends and engage in hobbies, as coping with the abuse takes more and more time. The shame of alcoholism in the family stops many family members from asking for help, instead pretending nothing is wrong. The emotional toll can be overwhelming. Children are especially sensitive.

When a loved one has a problem with alcohol

You may not immediately realize that someone you love has an alcohol problem. It may have started slowly, and your loved one might also have tried to hide the extent of the drinking from you. You might have gotten so used to the drinking that coping with it seems almost normal. It might actually feel normal if there was an alcoholic in the family growing up. The realization that there is something seriously wrong might be too painful to admit. Don't be ashamed, and you are not alone. Alcoholism affects millions of families, from every socioeconomic status, race and culture. There is help and support available.

What the person abusing alcohol might say if you confront them about their usage

"I can get sober any time I want to. I've done it lots of times". The key to recovery is *staying* sober, not constantly cycling through the process. Even if the alcoholic is able to resist for a little while, usually the cravings are too strong to resist during times of stress.

"Why do you exaggerate so much? I hardly drink at all!" Remember denial is a key part of alcoholism. The person abusing alcohol might actually believe they are not using as much as they are.

"It's your fault. If you wouldn't stress me out so much, maybe I wouldn't need to drink as often" It is never your fault that someone drinks too much. Even if they are feeling stressed, there are other coping skills they can choose to use.

What is involved in Recovery?

You cannot force someone you love to stop abusing alcohol. As much as you may want to, and as hard as it is seeing the effects, you cannot make someone stop drinking. The final choice is up to them. The right support can help you make positive choices for yourself, and balance encouraging your loved one to get help without losing yourself in the process.

Don't expect your loved one to be able to quit and stay sober without outside help. Your loved one will need help, support and new coping skills so that he or she will be able to resist cravings in a society where drinking is often glamorized. What's more, if your loved one has crossed the line from alcohol abuse to alcoholism, she or he has built up a tolerance to alcohol. Withdrawal symptoms can be unpleasant, painful, and even deadly.

Recovery will be an ongoing process. Someone who abused alcohol will not magically be a different person once sober. Alcohol use may have been masking painful feelings that will bubble up to the surface. It also takes time for the body and brain to recover from the effects of alcohol. Learning new coping skills and how to apply them in stressful situations is an ongoing process.

Finding support for yourself

A good place to start looking for support is through local support groups. Al-Anon is a free peer support group for families coping with alcoholism. Listening to others with the same challenges can be a tremendous source of comfort and support. Other sources of help and support include trusted friends, a therapist, or a pastor or rabbi.

Keeping your family safe

Dealing with a loved one's alcohol abuse can be emotionally draining and exhausting. But when the family is threatened with immediate violence, it's time for immediate action.

Alcohol abuse can lower inhibitions and increase the possibility of violence. Drinking may also become so important that activities like caring for a child fall by the wayside, increasing the chance of child neglect.

Starting Down the Road to Recovery

If you are abusing alcohol, even admitting that you may have a problem is a huge step. It takes tremendous strength and courage to admit that you are having trouble. Much as you may want to, don't try to quit alone. Without the right support, it is very easy to rationalize just one more drink, especially since alcohol is everywhere in our society. The road to sobriety is rewarding but challenging. If you take the time to build a support network and learn your triggers for drinking, you will greatly reduce the risk of relapse.

Much of that risk is inherited. Studies show that as much as 60 percent of the risk of alcohol-use disorders is genetic, said Dr. Marc Schuckit, professor of psychiatry at the University of California, San Diego, and director of the alcohol and drug treatment program at the Veterans Affairs-San Diego Healthcare System, who wrote the Lancet article.

The risk for alcoholism is four times greater for children of alcoholics, even those who are adopted by non-alcoholic

Families.

But people who have a genetically influenced disorder can control it by behaving responsibly. Just as someone at risk for diabetes shouldn't exacerbate the problem by becoming overweight, someone with a family history of alcoholism must avoid drinking too much.

Why is the risk so much greater in men than women? Psychiatrists point out that young women also have twice the rate of depression and anxiety that men do, and daughters of alcoholic fathers tend more toward depression than alcoholism.

Causes of alcoholism can be identified and when seeking treatment causes of alcoholism can help relieve feelings of blame and shame. Causes of alcoholism have been proven to be genetic in some cases, inherited from parents or grandparents. In other cases causes of alcoholism include the over abuse of alcohol until drinking no longer becomes a choice. This lack of choice stems from a change in the brain and body that become part of the causes of alcoholism. These physical causes of alcoholism create abnormal thinking patterns and personality characteristics.

The top expert associations in the medical, psychological and behavioral communities have agreed for years that alcoholism is a disease. Like any disease it can be encouraged by environmental and cultural factors. Particular diets of meats and fats have been linked to cancer and heart disease. Over consumption of sugar and lack of exercise can lead to diabetes and continual abuse of alcohol is one of the causes of alcoholism. On the other hand you have individuals who run 10 miles a week, don't smoke and eat right who still develop lung cancer or have heart attacks. These individuals most likely inherited a predisposition to the disease and no outside environmental force was going to change this fate. Same with alcoholism, if a drinkers parent or grandparent is an alcoholic, often they will sense that they are able to drink more than their friends. This immediate tolerance is not an asset to the pre-alcoholic who finds that he or she must drink more and more to receive the same effects that once took only a couple of drinks.

Some other causes of alcoholism are found in people who simply lack a certain amount of impulse control. Such personalities naturally want to feel good but have difficulty with delayed gratification. Scientists have identified the frontal brain lobe for much of this activity. For these personalities compulsive drinking is a habit out of control as they begin to use alcohol to escape from pressures and pain of daily living but can become consumed with drinking. It doesn't take long for social, family and job related problems to develop from the erratic behavior that drinking causes. The inability to meet obligations and criticism over drinking often can be used as excuses to drink even more. Certainly this cycle becomes difficult to break and spirals downward for millions of people every year. Alcoholics often excuse their excessive drinking by hanging out with other alcoholics or binge drinkers. Usually the causes of alcoholism are a combination of many of the factors described.

Happily there are many treatment facilities and organizations that specialize in recovery despite the causes of alcoholism. Rehabilitation centers address the physical, emotional and behavioral symptoms of the disease of alcoholism.

National Treatment Referral is such an organization that can put you in touch with a treatment facility that will serve your individual needs and desires. No matter what the cause of alcoholism, anyone with a drinking problem understands that they don't want to suffer with the consequences drinking has caused. Alcoholism is fully treatable and manageable but it takes work and a good program for recovery.

Call National Treatment Referral to discuss a program that will work for you. Our desire is to help anyone who seeks treatment for themselves or a loved one. The call is free and confidential. We look forward to hearing from you.

Question(s):

How does someone become an alcoholic/alcohol addict? How does alcoholism develop? What are the stages of development of alcoholism. What are the causes of alcoholism?

Answer:

You don't get dependent on alcohol just like that. It often takes years and usually begins with drinking for the effect.

Drinking for the effect

The motor for alcohol dependence is drinking for the effect. The drinker wants to change his mood to get rid of tensions, anxiety or grimness or to get more appreciation. Most people drink every now and then to change mood, but the real drinker-to-be strives for a more intense change of mood. He wants to experience a real turn, and wants to feel good again. When he does this several times, the problem is not solved and he runs the risk that his body gets used to the alcohol.

Getting used to the alcohol, or the development of tolerance

The body gets used to the alcohol. This is called the development of tolerance. At a certain moment, the drinker doesn't feel the effect of the alcohol anymore and he needs more and more. After all, his mood has to change.

Getting blackouts

When the drinker goes on and on and gets drunk regularly, he will eventually get blackouts. A blackout means that you miss a part of your intoxication. The next day you forget, for example, what you have said or how you got home. This startles the drinker in the beginning, but later on he deals with it indifferently. This is risky; he becomes blind to the disadvantages of alcohol abuse.

The development of problems related to alcohol use

Because of the heavy drinking problems arise. These can be physical problems, losing social contacts, problems at work or school, or financial problems. The question "do I drink because I have problems, or do I have problems because I drink?" becomes of current interest. You drink because you are using a bad problem solving method. More.

Getting withdrawal symptoms

In time, the body gets so used to alcohol that it will get with-drawal symptoms if it doesn't get a certain dose. You can start to tremble, sweat, sleep badly and feel restless.

Losing control

If the drinker keeps on drinking, it will get harder each time to drink less. The drinker resolves to reduce or quit after a few drinks, but can't stick to that.

Drinking maintains itself

At a certain moment, all these symptoms maintain the addic-tion. The drinker gets into a number of vicious circles. There are four circles:

1.   the pharmacological one: the withdrawal symptoms are suppressed by liquor. The withdrawal symptoms disappear temporarily, but come back with great intensity. For example, drinking alcohol to drive away feelings of restlessness.

2.   the mental one: Alcohol use leads to shame and guilt. The solution is sought in more alcohol, which only increases the shame and guilt.

3.   the social one: due to his drinking, the drinker gets involved in fights and gets isolated from the people around him. He can lose his partner and his job. Loneliness, fights and problems are reasons to start drinking again.

4.   the cerebral one: the use of alcohol causes brain damage. This can lead to having less resistance to the impulse to drink.

Like many other diseases, alcoholism affects you physically and mentally. Both your body and your mind have to be treated.

In addition to medicine, your doctor will probably recommend some psychosocial treatments. These treatments can help you change your behavior and cope with your problems without using alcohol. Examples of psychosocial treatments include Alcoholics Anonymous meetings, counseling, family therapy, group therapy, hospital treatment and other similar programs. There may be special centers in your area that offer this kind of treatment. Your doctor can refer you to the psychosocial treatment that is right for you.

Definition

Addiction is a dependence on a behavior or sub-stance that a person is powerless to stop. The term has been partially replaced by the word *dependence* for substance abuse. Addiction has been extended, however, to include mood-altering behaviors or activities. Some researchers speak of two types of addictions: substance addictions (for example, alcoholism, drug abuse, and smoking); and process addictions (for example, gambling, spending, shopping, eating, and sexual activity). There is a growing recognition that many addicts, such as polydrug abusers, are addicted to more than one sub-stance or process.

Description

Addiction is one of the most costly public health problems in the United States. It is a progressive syndrome, which means that it increases in severity over time unless it is treated. Substance abuse is characterized by frequent relapse, or return to the abused substance. Substance abusers often make repeated attempts to quit before they are successful.

In 1995 the economic cost of substance abuse in the United States exceeded $414 billion, with health care costs attributed to substance abuse estimated at more than $114 billion.

By eighth grade, 52% of adolescents have consumed alcohol, 41% have smoked tobacco, and 20% have smoked marijuana. Compared to females, males are almost four times as likely to be heavy drinkers, nearly one and a half more likely to smoke a pack or more of cigarettes daily, and twice as likely to smoke marijuana weekly. However, among adolescents these gender differences are decreasing. Although frequent use of tobacco, cocaine and heavy drinking appears to have remained stable in the 1990s, marijuana use increased.

In 1999, an estimated four million Americans over the age of 12 used prescription pain relievers, sedatives, and stimulants for "nonmedical" reasons during one month.

In the United States, 25% of the population regularly uses tobacco. Tobacco use reportedly kills 2.5 times as many people each year as alcohol and drug abuse combined. According to 1998 data from the World Health Organization, there were 1.1 billion smokers worldwide and 10,000 tobacco-related deaths per day. Furthermore, in the United States, 43% of children aged 2-11 years are exposed to environmental tobacco smoke, which has been implicated in sudden infant death syndrome,low birth weight, asthma, middle ear disease, pneumonia, cough, and upper respiratory infection.

Eating disorders, such as anorexia nervosa, bulimia nervosa, and binge eating, affect over five million American women and men. Fifteen percent of young women have substantially disordered attitudes toward eating and eating behaviors. More than 1,000 women die each year.

It is important to be working the 12 steps. However many people were not doing this and as a result they were relapsing. Now instead of working the 12 steps to feel better, people merely get on anti-depressants. Anti-depressants can be very beneficial in treating addictions provided that the anti-depressants are only used as prescribed. The major advantage is that the anti-depressants are not habit-forming. Therefore there is no danger of fueling the addiction or cross-addiction.

In looking at the pharmacological treatments for addiction, it is found the more effective treatments are with cognitive approaches and behavioral modification approaches. The reason that the cognitive approaches are more effective is that a person's thinking patterns have to be restructured so that what used to be fun is no longer fun and what used to be boring now becomes fun. This is achieved by the transformation of one's thoughts from a more negative to a more positive way of thinking that is more conducive to peace of mind and less conflicting. That is to say, that instead of life being full of conflicts and problems, life now becomes more palatable, enjoyable, exciting, and nourishing. This is brought about by cognitive restructuring. In fact, the AA way of life is brought about by a process restructuring.

This brings us to our original premise or what this book is all about. That is to say why is it that some people are able to drink alcohol with no problem. These people are able to get along well in life with no foreseeable problem as far as alcohol is concerned. Many researchers believe that the answer lies in the mental cognition of different individuals. That is to say that alcoholics have a malfunction when it comes to the ability to think straight. It is often said of alcoholics that their thinker is broken. Alcoholics tend to think in more negative patterns. If the glass is half fill or half empty. Alcoholics tend to see the glass as half empty. Where other people tend to see the same glass as half full. These negative cognitions or thinking patterns tend to make a person look for some relief from this type of thinking. This is one of the main reasons that the alcoholic continues to use substances. After drinking alcohol and doing drugs the addict or alcoholic's mind becomes warped. The thought patterns line up so that the addict is constantly seeking a drink without even being aware of it many times. For instance a person will find themselves dating only those persons that will allow them to drink. A person will take certain jobs if they can drink without impunity. There is one alcoholic that quit teaching school because he could not drink. This same alcoholic began working on an assembly line because he was permitted to drink without losing his job. A person finds himself thinking constantly about getting a drink of alcohol. Every waking moment is spent thinking on plotting to get a drink of alcohol.

METABOLISM: In discussing the Etiology of alcoholism, we come to the next topic, which is the etiology of alcoholism. When all of this alcohol is ingested, it has to be metabolized or broken down. That we believe is the central core that separates alcoholics from non-alcoholics. The different ways that the body breaks down the alcohol is what determines addiction.

Metabolism is the body's process of converting ingested substances to other compounds. Metabolism results in some substances becoming more, and some less, toxic than those originally ingested. Metabolism involves a number of processes, one of which is referred to as oxidation. Through oxidation, alcohol is detoxified and removed from the blood, preventing the alcohol from accumulating and destroying cells and organs. A minute amount of alcohol escapes metabolism and is excreted unchanged the breath and in urine. Until all the alcohol consumed has been metabolized, it is distributed throughout the body, affecting the brain and other tissues

FOOD: A number of factors influence the absorption process, including the presence of food and the type of food in the gastrointestinal tract when alcohol is consume (2,6). The rate at which alcohol is absorbed depends on how quickly the stomach empties its contents into the intestine. The higher the dietary fat content, the more time this emptying will require and the longer the process of absorption will take. One study found that subjects who drank alcohol after a meal that included fat, protein, and carbohydrates absorbed the alcohol about three times more slowly than when they consumed alcohol on an empty stomach (7).

GENDER: Women absorb and metabolize alcohol differently from men. They have higher BAC's after consuming the same amount of alcohol as men and are more susceptible to alcoholic liver disease, heart muscle damage (8), and brain damage (9). The difference in BAC's between women and men has been attributed to women's smaller amount of body water, likened to dropping the same amount of alcohol into a smaller pail of water (10). An additional factor contributing to the difference in BAC's may be that women have lower activity of the alcohol metabolizing enzyme ADH (Alcohol Dehydrogenase) in the stomach, causing a larger proportion of ingested alcohol to reach the blood. The combination of these factors may render women more vulnerable than men to alcohol-induced liver and heart damage.

SEX HORMONES: Alcohol metabolism alters the balance of reproductive hormones in men and women. In men, alcohol metabolism contributes to testicular injury and impairs testosterone synthesis and sperm production. In a study of normal healthy men who received 220 grams of alcohol daily for 4 weeks, testosterone levels declined after only 5 days and continued to fall throughout the study period. Prolonged testosterone deficiency may contribute to feminization in males, for example, breast enlargement. In addition, alcohol may interfere with normal sperm structure and movement by inhibiting the metabolism of vitamin A, which is essential for sperm development. In women, alcohol metabolism may This many times leads to death. The addiction is progressive. That means that the more a person uses the drug, the deeper the depression or the more pronounced the withdrawal process will be. So therefore, one who has used cocaine for an extended period of time, becomes very suicidal as a result the consequences surrounding the use of the drug. Many overdoses are actually suicide attempts. Anti-Depressants have served to aid in the prevention of suicides involving addiction. Therefore anti-depressants have proven to be an excellent panacea in treating cocaine addiction and withdrawal symptoms. The anti-depressants serve as a buffer and help the cocaine addict through the crucial period when the cravings are so great and so pronounced.

By treating the depression, the addict is actually able to abstain from the use of cocaine and other substances for long periods and many times for good. Treating the depression has proven to be the missing formula that has been needed for years in treating addictions. Depression is such a debilitating feeling that a person will do almost anything to escape this awful feeling of being down in the dumps. The feeling is similar to being in a tunnel that has no means of escape or any semblance of light. Treating the depression has proven to be a very effective formula for treating addictions.

For many years, in treating addictions, it has been understood that long term sobriety was brought about by attending AA meetings.

In medical terminology, an **addiction** is a state in which the body relies on a substance for normal functioning and develops physical dependence, as in drug addiction. When the drug or substance on which someone is dependent is suddenly removed, it will cause withdrawal, a characteristic set of signs and symptoms. Addiction is generally associated with increased drug tolerance. In physiological terms, addiction is not necessarily associated with substance abuse since this form of addiction can result from using medication as prescribed by a doctor.

The term *addiction* is also sometimes applied to compulsions that are not substance-related, such as problem gambling and computer addiction. In these kinds of common usages, the term *addiction* is used to describe a recurring compulsion by an individual to engage in some specific activity, despite harmful consequences to the individual's health, mental state or social life.

Prior to the latter half of the 20th Century, addiction was primarily a pharmacological term that referred to the process of developing drug tolerance so that more of a drug was required, more frequently, for the same effect to occur. However, with the founding of Alcoholics Anonymous in 1935, the allergy concept eventually morphed into the disease-model of addiction was proposed, based on the work of Dr. William Duncan Silkworth, and began to gather support in the professional community, amongst medical and social services workers, and amongst addicts themselves. The disease-model concept led to a definition of addiction based on the continued use of alcohol or drugs despite negative consequences for the user. This latter definition is now thought of as a disease state by the medical community. Morse and Flavin summarise the disease-model definition of addiction commonly utilized by treatment centers and substance abuse counselors:

Addiction is a primary, progressive, chronic disease with genetic, psychosocial, and environmental factors influencing its development and manifestations. The disease is often progressive and fatal. It is characterized by impaired control over use of the substance, preoccupation with the substance, use of the substance despite adverse consequences, and distortions in thinking.[2]

In the latter half of the 20th Century, the twelve-step program began to be applied to a wide range of problem behaviours, many never previously identified as addictions. For example, during this process the establishment of Overeaters Anonymous in 1960 led to the identification of an associated concept of food addiction[3] [4]and the establishment of Sex and Love Addicts Anonymous in 1977 led to the identification of the concept of sexual addiction-- However, although these terms are widely used in the recovery movement, and by commentators on that movement, neither of them are widely accepted by members of the professional communities working in the fields of addiction.

Definition

Not all doctors agree on the exact nature of addiction or dependency, however the <u>biopsychosocial model</u> is generally accepted in scientific fields as the most comprehensive theorem for addiction. Historically, addiction has been defined with regard solely to psychoactive substances (for example <u>alcohol</u>, <u>tobacco</u> and other <u>drugs</u>) which cross the <u>blood-brain barrier</u> once ingested, temporarily altering the chemical milieu of the brain. Many people, both psychology professionals and laypersons, now feel that there should be accommodation made to include psychological dependency on such things as <u>gambling</u>, <u>food</u>, <u>sex</u>, <u>pornography</u>, <u>computers</u>, <u>work</u>, <u>exercise</u>, spiritual obsession (as opposed to religious devotion), <u>cutting</u> and <u>shopping</u> so these behaviors count as 'addictions' as well and cause <u>guilt</u>, <u>shame</u>, <u>fear</u>, <u>hopelessness</u>, <u>failure</u>, <u>rejection</u>, <u>anxiety</u>, or <u>humiliation</u> symptoms associated with, among other medical conditions, <u>depression</u> and <u>epilepsy</u>. Although, the above mentioned are things or tasks which, when used or performed, do not fit into the traditional view of addiction and may be better defined as an <u>obsessive-compulsive disorder</u>, <u>withdrawal</u> symptoms may occur with abatement of such behaviors. It is said by those who adhere to a traditionalist view that these withdrawal-like symptoms are not strictly reflective of an addiction, but rather of a behavioral disorder. nfirmed repeatedly. Modern research into addiction is generally focused on <u>Dopaminergic pathways</u>. There is great and sometimes heated debate around the definition of addiction with parties falling into two main camps the <u>Disease model of addiction</u> .

In the <u>United States</u>, <u>physical dependence</u>, <u>abuse</u> of, and <u>withdrawal</u> from <u>drugs</u> and other <u>substances</u> is outlined in the <u>Diagnostic and Statistical Manual of Mental Disorders</u> (DSM-IV TR). It does not use the word 'addiction' at all. It has instead a section about <u>Substance dependence</u>:

"**Substance dependence** When an individual persists in use of alcohol or other drugs despite problems related to use of the substance, <u>substance dependence</u> may be diagnosed. Compulsive and repetitive use may result in tolerance to the effect of the drug and withdrawal symptoms when use is reduced or stopped. This, along with <u>Substance Abuse</u> are considered Substance Use Disorders..."[16]

The medical community now makes a careful theoretical distinction between *physical dependence* (characterized by symptoms of <u>withdrawal</u>) and *psychological dependence* (or simply *addiction*). Addiction is now narrowly defined as "uncontrolled, compulsive use"; if there is no harm being suffered by, or damage done to, the patient or another party, then clinically it may be considered <u>compulsive</u>, but to the definition of some it is not categorized as 'addiction'. In practice, the two kinds of addiction are not always easy to distinguish. Addictions often have both physical and psychological components.

In modern pain management with opioids physical dependence is nearly universal. While opiates are essential in the treatment of acute pain, the benefit of this class of medication in chronic pain is not well proven. Clearly, there are those who would not function well without opiate treatment; on the other hand, many states are noting significant increases in non-intentional deaths related to opiate use. High-quality, long-term studies are needed to better delineate the risks and benefits of chronic opiate use. Michael Jackson's fate was basically determine because of pain management from being severely burned. This is estimated to have lead to a hug opiate addiction. This leads to the harm-reduction theory. "Is it better to be treated with opiates to relieve pain or to be in severe paid 24 hours a day." We'll let you be the judge. This can be a good discussion topic.

[edit] **Physical dependency**

Physical dependence on a substance is defined by the appearance of characteristic withdrawal symptoms when the substance is suddenly discontinued. Opiates, amphetamines, benzodiazepines, barbiturates, alcohol and nicotine induce physical dependence. On the other hand, some categories of substances share this property and are still not considered addictive: cortisone, beta blockers and most antidepressants are examples. So, while physical dependency can be a major factor in the psychology of addiction and most often becomes a primary motivator in the continuation of an addiction, the initial primary attribution of an addictive substance is usually its ability to induce pleasure, although with continued use the goal is not so much to induce pleasure as it is to relieve the anxiety caused by the absence of a given addictive substance, causing it to become used compulsively. An example of this is nicotine; A cigarette can be described as pleasurable, but is in fact fulfilling the physical addiction of the user, and therefore, is achieving pleasurable feelings relative to his/her previous state of physical withdrawal. Further, the physical dependency of the nicotine addict on the substance itself becomes an overwhelming factor in the continuation of use.

The speed with which a given individual becomes addicted to various substances varies with the substance, the frequency of use, the means of ingestion, the intensity of pleasure or euphoria, and the individual's genetic and psychological susceptibility. Some people may exhibit alcoholic tendencies from the moment of first intoxication, while most people can drink socially without ever becoming addicted. Opioid dependent individuals have different responses to even low doses of opioids than the majority of people, although this may be due to a variety of other factors, as opioid use heavily stimulates pleasure-inducing neurotransmitters in the brain. Nonetheless, because of these variations, in addition to the adoption and twin studies that have been well replicated, much of the medical community is satisfied that addiction is in part genetically moderated. That is, one's genetic makeup may regulate how susceptible one is to a substance and how easily one may become psychologically attached to a pleasurable routine.

Eating disorders are complicated pathological mental illnesses and thus are not the same as addictions described in this article. Eating disorders, which some argue are not addictions at all, are driven by a multitude of factors, most of which are highly different than the factors behind addictions described in this article. It has been reported, however, that patients with eating disorders can successfully be treated with the same non-pharmacological protocols used in patients with chemical addiction disorders. Gambling is another potentially addictive behavior with some biological overlap.

Psychological dependency

Psychological dependency is a dependency of the mind, and leads to psychological withdrawal symptoms (such as cravings, irritability, insomnia, depression, anorexia, etc). Addiction can in theory be derived from any rewarding behaviour, and is believed to be strongly associated with the dopaminergic system of the brain's reward system (as in the case of cocaine and amphetamines). Some claim that it is a habitual means to avoid undesired activity, but typically it is only so to a clinical level in individuals who have emotional, social, or psychological dysfunctions (psychological addiction is defined as such).

A person who is physically dependent, but not psychologically dependent can have their dose slowly dropped until they are no longer dependent. However, if that person is psychologically dependent, they are still at serious risk for relapse into abuse and subsequent physical dependence,

Psychological dependence does not have to be limited only to substances; even activities and behavioral patterns can be considered addictions, if they become uncontrollable, e.g. problem gambling, Internet addiction, computer addiction, sexual addiction / pornography addiction, eating, self-injury, or work addiction.

Addiction and drug control legislation in the U.S.

Most countries have legislation which brings various drugs and drug-like substances under the control of licensing systems. Typically this legislation covers any or all of the opiates, amphetamines, cannabinoids, cocaine, barbiturates, hallucinogens (tryptamines, LSD, phencyclidine(PCP), psilocybin) and a variety of more modern synthetic drugs, and unlicensed production, supply or possession may be a criminal offense.

Usually, however, drug classification under such legislation is not related simply to addictiveness. The substances covered often have very different addictive properties. Some are highly prone to cause physical dependency, whilst others rarely cause any form of compulsive need whatsoever. Typically nicotine (in the form of tobacco) is regulated extremely loosely, if at all, although it is well-known as one of the most addictive substances ever discovered.

Also, although the legislation may be justifiable on moral grounds to some, it can make addiction or dependency a much more serious issue for the individual. Reliable supplies of a drug become difficult to secure as illegally produced substances may have contaminants. Withdrawal from the substances or associated contaminants can cause additional health issues and the individual becomes vulnerable to both criminal abuse and legal punishment. Criminal elements that can be involved in the profitable trade of such substances can also cause physical harm to users.

Addiction Recovery Process

- Acute intoxication and/or <u>withdrawal</u> potential
- Biomedical conditions or complications
- Emotional/behavioral conditions or complications
- Treatment acceptance/resistance
- <u>Relapse</u> potential
- <u>Recovery environment</u>

Some medical systems, including those of at least 15 states of the United States, refer to an <u>Addiction Severity Index</u> to assess the severity of problems related to substance use. The index assesses problems in six areas: medical, employment/support, alcohol and other drug use, legal, family/social, and psychiatric.

While addiction or dependency is related to seemingly uncontrollable urges, and arguably could have roots in genetic predispositions, treatment of dependency is conducted by a wide range of medical and allied professionals, including <u>Addiction Medicine</u> specialists, psychiatrists, and appropriately trained nurses, social workers, and counselors. Early treatment of acute withdrawal often includes medical <u>detoxification</u>, which can include doses of <u>anxiolytics</u> or narcotics to reduce symptoms of withdrawal. An experimental drug, <u>ibogaine</u>,[20] is also proposed to treat withdrawal and craving. Alternatives to medical detoxification include <u>acupuncture detoxification</u>. In chronic opiate addiction, a surrogate drug such as <u>methadone</u> is sometimes offered as a form of <u>opiate replacement therapy</u>. But treatment approaches universal focus on the individual's ultimate choice to pursue an alternate course of action.

Therapists often classify patients with chemical dependencies as either interested or not interested in changing. Treatments usually involve planning for specific ways to avoid the addictive stimulus, and therapeutic interventions intended to help a client learn healthier ways to find satisfaction. Clinical leaders in recent years have attempted to tailor intervention approaches to specific influences that affect addictive behavior, using therapeutic interviews in an effort to discover factors that led a person to embrace unhealthy, addictive sources of pleasure or relief from pain.

Several explanations (or "models") have been presented to explain addiction. These divide, more or less, into the models which stress biological or genetic causes for addiction, and those which stress social or purely psychological causes. Of course there are also many models which attempt to see addiction as both a physiological *and* a psycho-social phenomenon.

- The <u>disease model of addiction</u> holds that addiction is a <u>disease</u>, coming about as a result of either the impairment of <u>neurochemical</u> or <u>behavioral</u> processes, or of some combination of the two. Within this model, addictive disease is treated by specialists in <u>Addiction Medicine</u>. Within the field of medicine, the <u>American Medical Association</u>, National Association of Social Workers, and <u>American Psychological Association</u> all have policies which are predicated on the theory that addictive processes represent a disease state. Most treatment approaches, as well, are based on the idea that dependencies are behavioral dysfunctions, and, therefore, contain, at least to some extent, elements of physical or mental disease. Organizations such as the <u>American Society of Addiction Medicine</u> believe the research-based evidence for addiction's status as a disease is overwhelming.

- The <u>pleasure</u> *model* proposed by professor <u>Nils Bejerot</u>. Addiction "is an emotional fixation (sentiment) acquired through learning, which intermittently or continually expresses itself in purposeful, stereotyped behavior with the character and force of a natural drive, aiming at a specific pleasure or the avoidance of a specific discomfort." "The pleasure mechanism may be stimulated in a number of ways and give rise to a strong fixation on repetitive behavior. Stimulation with drugs is only one of many ways, but one of the simplest, strongest,and often also the most destructive" "If the pleasure stimulation becomes so strong that it captivates an individual with the compulsion and force characteristic of natural drives, then there exists...an addiction" The pleasure model is used as one of the reason for <u>zero tolerance</u> for use of illicit drugs

- The <u>genetic</u> *model* posits a genetic predisposition to certain behaviors. It is frequently noted that certain addictions "run in the family," and while researchers continue to explore the extent of genetic influence, many researchers argue that there is strong evidence that genetic predisposition is often a factor in dependency.

- The <u>experiential</u> *model* devised by <u>Stanton Peele</u> argues that addictions occur with regard to experiences generated by various involvements, whether drug-induced or not. This model is in opposition to the disease, genetic, and neurobiological approaches. Among other things, it proposes that addiction is both more temporary or situational than the disease model claims, and is often outgrown through natural processes.

- The <u>opponent-process</u> *model* generated by Richard Soloman states that for every psychological event A will be followed by its opposite psychological event B. For example, the pleasure one experiences from <u>heroin</u> is followed by an opponent process of withdrawal, or the terror of jumping out of an airplane is rewarded with intense pleasure when the parachute opens. This model is related to the opponent process color theory. If you look at the color red then quickly look at a gray area you will see green. There are many examples of opponent processes in the nervous system including taste, motor movement, touch, vision, and hearing. Opponent-processes occurring at the sensory level may translate "down-stream" into addictive or habit-forming behavior.

• The <u>cultural</u> *model* recognizes that the influence of culture is a strong determinant of whether or not individuals fall prey to certain addictions. For example, alcoholism is rare among <u>Saudi Arabians</u>, where obtaining alcohol is difficult and using alcohol is prohibited. In North America, on the other hand, the incidence of <u>gambling</u> addictions soared in the last two decades of the 20th century, mirroring the growth of the gaming industry. Half of all patients diagnosed as alcoholic are born into families where alcohol is used heavily, suggesting that familiar influence, genetic factors, or more likely both, play a role in the development of addiction. What also needs to be noted is that when people don't gain a sense of moderation through their development they can be just as likely, if not more, to abuse substances than people born into alcoholic families.

• The <u>moral</u> *model* states that addictions are the result of human weakness, and are defects of <u>character</u>. Those who advance this model do not accept that there is any biological basis for addiction. They often have scant sympathy for people with serious addictions, believing either that a person with greater moral strength could have the force of will to break an addiction, or that the addict demonstrated a great moral failure in the first place by starting the addiction. The moral model is widely applied to dependency on illegal substances, perhaps purely for social or political reasons, but is no longer widely considered to have any therapeutic value. Elements of the moral model, especially a focus on individual choices, have found enduring roles in other approaches to the treatment of dependencies.

- The <u>habit</u> *model* or "<u>life-process model</u>" proposed by <u>Thomas Szasz</u> questions the very concept of "addiction." He argues that addiction is a metaphor, and that the only reason to make the distinction between habit and addiction "is to persecute somebody." However, the nature of this metaphor is unclear, and the list of groups that rejects Szasz's opinion that mental illness is a myth includes the <u>American Psychiatric Association</u> (APA) and the <u>National Institute of Mental Health</u> (NIMH).

- Finally, the *blended model* attempts to consider elements of all other models in developing a therapeutic approach to dependency. It holds that the mechanism of dependency is different for different individuals, and that each case must be considered on its own merits.

Neurobiological basis

he development of addiction is thought to involve a simultaneous process of 1) increased focus on and engagement in a particular behavior and 2) the attenuation or "shutting down" of other behaviors. For example, under certain experimental circumstances such as social <u>deprivation</u> and boredom, animals allowed the unlimited ability to self-administer certain psychoactive drugs will show such a strong preference that they will forgo food, sleep, and sex for continued access. The neuro-anatomical correlate of this is that the brain regions involved in driving goal-directed behavior grow increasingly selective for particular motivating stimuli and rewards, to the point that the brain regions involved in the inhibition of behavior can no longer effectively send "stop" signals. A good analogy is to imagine flooring the gas pedal in a car with very bad brakes. In this case, the limbic system is thought to be the major "driving force" and the orbitofrontal cortex is the substrate of the top-down inhibition.

A specific portion of the limbic circuit known as the mesolimbic dopaminergic system is hypothesized to play an important role in translation of motivation to motor behavior- and reward-related learning in particular. It is typically defined as the ventral tegmental area (VTA), the nucleus accumbens, and the bundle of dopamine-containing fibers that are connecting them. This system is commonly implicated in the seeking out and consumption of rewarding stimuli or events, such as sweet-tasting foods or sexual interaction. However, its importance to addiction research goes beyond its role in "natural" motivation: while the specific site or mechanism of action may differ, all known drugs of abuse have the common effect in that they elevate the level of dopamine in the nucleus accumbens. This may happen directly, such as through blockade of the dopamine re-uptake mechanism (see cocaine). It may also happen indirectly, such as through stimulation of the dopamine-containing neurons of the VTA that synapse onto neurons in the accumbens (see opiates). The euphoric effects of drugs of abuse are thought to be a direct result of the acute increase in accumbal dopamine.[26]

The human body has a natural tendency to maintain homeostasis, and the central nervous system is no exception. Chronic elevation of dopamine will result in a decrease in the number of dopamine receptors available in a process known as downregulation. The decreased number of receptors changes the permeability of the cell membrane located post-synaptically, such that the post-synaptic neuron is less excitable- i.e.: less able to respond to chemical signaling with an electrical impulse, or action potential. It is hypothesized that this dulling of the responsiveness of the brain's reward pathways contributes to the inability to feel pleasure, known as <u>anhedonia</u>, often observed in addicts. The increased requirement for dopamine to maintain the same electrical activity is the basis of both <u>physiological tolerance</u> and <u>withdrawal</u> associated with addiction.

Downregulation can be classically conditioned. If a behavior consistently occurs in the same environment or contingently with a particular cue, the brain will adjust to the presence of the conditioned cues by decreasing the number of available receptors in the absence of the behavior. It is thought that many drug overdoses are not the result of a user taking a higher dose than is typical, but rather that the user is administering the same dose in a new environment.

In cases of physical dependency on <u>depressants</u> of the <u>central nervous system</u> such as <u>opioids</u>, <u>barbiturates</u>, or alcohol, the absence of the substance can lead to symptoms of severe physical discomfort. Withdrawal from alcohol or sedatives such as barbiturates or <u>benzodiazepines</u> (valium-family) can result in seizures and even death. By contrast, withdrawal from opioids, which can be extremely uncomfortable, is rarely if ever life-threatening. In cases of dependence and withdrawal, the body has become so dependent on high concentrations of the particular chemical that it has stopped producing its own natural versions (endogenous ligands) and instead produces opposing chemicals. When the addictive substance is withdrawn, the effects of the opposing chemicals can become overwhelming. For example, chronic use of sedatives (alcohol, <u>barbiturates</u>, or benzodiazepines) results in higher chronic levels of stimulating <u>neurotransmitters</u> such as glutamate. Very high levels of glutamate kill nerve cells, a phenomenon called excitatory neurotoxicity.

Criticism

A strong form of criticism comes from <u>Thomas Szasz</u>, who denies that addiction is a psychiatric problem. In many of his works, he argues that addiction is a choice, and that a drug addict is one who simply prefers a socially taboo substance rather than, say, a low risk lifestyle. In *Our Right to Drugs*, Szasz cites the biography of <u>Malcolm X</u> to corroborate his economic views towards addiction: Malcolm claimed that quitting cigarettes was harder than shaking his <u>heroin</u> addiction. Szasz postulates that humans always have a choice, and it is foolish to call someone an 'addict' just because they prefer a <u>drug</u> induced <u>euphoria</u> to a more popular and socially welcome lifestyle.

Szasz is not alone in questioning the standard view of addiction. Professor John Booth Davies at the <u>University of Strathclyde</u> has argued in his book *The Myth of Addiction* that 'people take drugs because they want to and because it makes sense for them to do so given the choices available' as opposed to the view that 'they are compelled to by the pharmacology of the drugs they take'. He uses an adaptation of <u>attribution theory</u> (what he calls the theory of functional attributions) to argue that the statement 'I am addicted to drugs' is functional, rather than veridical. <u>Stanton Peele</u> has put forward similar views.

Experimentally, Bruce K. Alexander used the classic experiment of <u>Rat Park</u> to show that 'addicted' behaviour in rats only occurred when the rats had no other options. When other options and behavioural opportunities were put in place, the rats soon showed far more complex behaviours.

Vocabulary lists

- Addiction recovery groups -12-Step Groups such as Alcoholic's Anonymous, Narcotics Anonymous, and Cocaine Anonymous.

- Addiction medicine – Addictionologist is one who specializes in treating addiction.

- Akrasia – characterized by weakness of willpower

- Alcoholism –The repeated use of alcohol ingestion resulting in tolerance, and withdrawal symptoms when the alcohol if the use is suspended.

- Alcohol withdrawal syndrome – caused by the cessation or the reduction of alcohol

- Benzodiazepine withdrawal syndrome –caused by the cessation or the reduction of benzodiazepines.

- Codependence – a dysfunctional relationship pattern in which an individual is psychologically dependent on someone else.

- Cold turkey- an abrupt cessation of the use of drugs, particularly opiates, without cushioning the impact by use of other drugs or tranquilizers.

- Computer addiction- addicted to constantly being on the computer.

- Conditioned place preference – a technique for determining if experience with cetain stimuli renders the splae where that experience occurred reiforcin.

- Cue reactivity is a phenomenon of addiction found in numerous laboratory studies showing that drug addicts have significant physiological and subjective reactions to presentations of drug-related stimuli.

- Disease model of addiction –This model also known as the medical model of addiction. This model states that addiction is caused by a genetic predisposition that causes the addiction.

• Drug addiction -widely considered a <u>pathological state</u>. The disorder of <u>addiction</u> involves the progression of acute <u>drug use</u> to the development of drug-seeking behavior, the vulnerability to relapse, and the decreased, slowed ability to respond to naturally rewarding stimuli. The <u>Diagnostic and Statistical Manual of Mental Disorders, Fourth Edition</u> (DSM-IV) has categorized three stages of addiction: preoccupation/anticipation, binge/intoxication, and withdrawal/negative affect. These stages are characterized, respectively, everywhere by constant cravings and preoccupation with obtaining the substance; using more of the substance than necessary to experience the intoxicating effects; and experiencing tolerance, withdrawal symptoms, and decreased motivation for normal life activities.

<u>Drug Interventions Programme</u> – Drug intervention programs offer counseling, eductation and detoxification if needed. Intervention is the best way to make help available to those struggling with an addiction. 92% of those intervened on go to treatment and have the opportunity to change their lives.

<u>Intervention:</u> a process by which the harmful, progressive and destructive effects of chemical dependency are interrupted and the chemically dependent person is helped to stop using mood-altering chemical, and to develop new, healthier ways to coping with his or her needs and problems.

<u>Mood Altering:</u> a drug that causes one's mood to change.

Obsession: a persistent pre-occupation with an often unreasonable act.

Psychoactive: mind or mood altering.

Psychotherapy: the psychological treatment of mental, emotional, and nervous   disorders.

Recidivism: a tendency to relapse into a previous condition or mode of behavior.

Recidivist: one who relapses.

Stimulant: an agent that temporarily produces or arouses physiological organic activity.

Korsakoff syndrome, or Korsakoff psychosis, tends to develop as Wernicke's symptoms diminish. It involves impairment of memory out of proportion to problems with other cognitive functions. Patients often attempt to hide their poor memory by confabulating. The patient will create detailed, believable stories about experiences or situations to cover gaps in memory. This is not usually a deliberate attempt to deceive because the patient often believes what he is saying to be true. It can occur whether or not the thiamine deficiency was related to alcoholism and with other types of brain damage.

Mood Altering: a drug that causes one's mood to change.

Obsession: a persistent pre-occupation with an often unreasonable act.

Physical dependence-refers to a state resulting from chronic use of a drug that has produced tolerance and where negative physical symptom of withdrawal result from abrupt discontinuation or dosage reduction. Physical dependence can develop from low-dose therapeutic use of certain medications as well as misuse of recreational drugs such as alcohol. The higher the dose used typically the worse the physical dependence and thus the worse the withdrawal syndrome. Withdrawal syndromes can last days, weeks or months or occasionally longer and will vary according to the dose, the type of drug used and the individual person.

<u>Psychoactive:</u> mind or mood altering.

<u>Psychotherapy:</u> the psychological treatment of mental, emotional, and nervous   disorders.

<u>Recidivism:</u> a tendency to relapse into a previous condition or mode

<u>Wierneke's Disease-Wernicke-Korsakoff</u> syndrome- is commonly known as "Wet Brain". This is a brain disorder involving loss of specific brain functions caused by a thiamine deficiency as a result of alcoholism. It may also include symptoms caused by alcohol withdrawal. The cause is generally attributed to malnutrition, especially lack of vitamin B1 (thiamine), which commonly accompanies habitual alcohol use or alcoholism. Heavy alcohol use interferes with the metabolism of thiamine, so even in the unusual cases where alcoholics are eating a balanced diet while drinking heavily, the metabolic problem persists because most of the thiamine is not absorbed.

10 Steps of an Intervention

Step 1 – Call a professional to do the intervention.

Step 2 - Placement with an interventionist

Upon clinical assessment of your individual needs, you will be matched with an appropriate interventionist.

Step 3 - Outline treatment options

The interventionist will outline specific treatment options according to your unique needs (location, clinical matters, medical coverage, etc). Once we have determined the appropriate outlet, our team will take care of admissions details and necessary travel arrangements.

Step 4 - Outline a plan of action

Through a series of one-on-one meetings and/or telephone conversations, your interventionist will guide you and others involved through the process of organizing a professionally facilitated, effective intervention.

Step 5 - Pre-intervention meeting

Your interventionist will fly or drive to your location for the pre-intervention meeting. This meeting is typically scheduled during the late afternoon or evening and lasts an average of three to four hours. During this meeting, we talk about the disease of addiction and its impact on family, friends, co-workers and others. We discuss what the treatment course and recovery process will involve and, finally, under the guidance of your interventionist, we will prepare and rehearse written statements to share with your loved one during the intervention.

Step 6 - Intervention

Interventions are typically scheduled for the morning immediately following the pre-intervention meeting. The intervention usually takes about one to one-and-a-half hours. An intervention is a structured, solution-focused process that consist of a group of close friends, family members, co-workers, colleagues, spiritual advisors, etc., who come together in a caring and non-judgmental manner to present their observations and concerns regarding an addict's behavior.

Step 7 - Treatment admissions

If the individual accepts help, he or she is immediately escorted to the appropriate treatment outlet. Your interventionist will work with the treatment staff in regards to the critical information gained during the intervention process so that treatment staff can get a jump-start on the assessment and treatment planning process.

Step 8 - Post-intervention consultation

After the intervention, our counselors and interventionists will be available for unlimited, free consultations, whether or not the individual chooses to accept help for his or her problem. We also assist in helping you start your own path of recovery and healing.

Step 9 - Post-treatment services

Support immediately following treatment significantly increases the probability of abstinence and aids in the major transition from treatment to independent, sober living. The goal of our re-entry program is to provide intense, individualized care during this critical transitional period so that your loved one can begin to develop a healthy, satisfying and productive life in sobriety. These highly individualized services are offered at additional cost.

Step 10 - Congratulations on taking the first step toward recovery.

E. Morton Jellinek -was a biostatistician, physiologist, and an alcoholism researcher. He was born in New York City and died at the desk of his study at Stanford University on 22 October 1963. He was fluent in nine languages and could communicate in four others. Addiction researcher Griffith Edwards holds that, in his opinion, Jellinek's *The Disease Concept of Alcoholism* was a work of outstanding scholarship based on a careful consideration of the available evidence.

<u>Food addiction</u> -Food addiction is a contemporary term used to describe a pathological disorder; the compulsive, excessive craving for and consumption of food. This condition is not only manifested by the abnormal intake of food, but the intake and craving for foods that are, in themselves, harmful to the individual. While society and the medical profession have readily understood alcoholism and drug abuse, it is only in recent years that there is an equal acceptance of the fact that persons may be addicted to food in the same way.

<u>Higher order desire</u> -Higher-order volitions are potentially more often guided by long-term convictions and <u>reasoning</u>. A first-order volition is a desire about anything else, such as to own a new car, to meet the pope, or to drink alcohol. Second-order volitions to parallel these examples would be to desire to want to own a new car; to desire indifference about meeting the pope; or to desire to not want to drink alcohol. A higher-order volition can go unfulfilled due to uncontrolled lower-order volitions.

An example for a failure to follow higher-order volitions is the drug addict who takes drugs even though he would like to quit taking drugs. According to <u>Harry Frankfurt</u> the drug addict has established <u>free will</u>, in respect to that single aspect, when his higher-order volition to stop wanting drugs determines the precedence of his changing, action determining desires either to take drugs or not to take drugs.

<u>Junkie</u>- a slang for a drug addict, especially a heroin addict.

<u>Intervention:</u> a process by which the harmful, progressive and destructive effects of chemical dependency are interrupted and the chemically dependent person is helped to stop using mood-altering chemical, and to develop new, healthier ways to coping with his or her needs and problems.

Life-process model of addiction -The **life-process model of addiction** is the view that addiction is not a disease but rather a habitual response and a source of gratification and security that can be understood only in the context of social relationships and experiences.

Love addiction -Love Addiction consists of three components: Romance, Relationship and Sexual Addiction. Love addiction is often perceived to be "less serious" than other process addictions i.e. compulsive sexual addictions, eating disorders or self-harm / mutilation addictions. Perhaps because it sounds "softer." In reality it is extremely painful. and can be very dangerous to both the addict and their partners. Many suicides, murders, stalkings, rapes and other crimes of passion have their roots in this addiction. Our culture has traditionally glorified love addiction with the notion that we fall in love and live "happily ever after." This ignores the groundwork that relationships require. Many love relationships depicted in the media are really love addicted relationships. (See Romeo and Juliet as an example - not a very happy ending, huh?)

Korsakoff syndrome, or Korsakoff psychosis, tends to develop as Wernicke's symptoms diminish. It involves impairment of memory out of proportion to problems with other cognitive functions. Patients often attempt to hide their poor memory by confabulating. The patient will create detailed, believable stories about experiences or situations to cover gaps in memory. This is not usually a deliberate attempt to deceive because the patient often believes what he is saying to be true. It can occur whether or not the thiamine deficiency was related to alcoholism and with other types of brain damage.

Mood Altering: a drug that causes one's mood to change.

Obsession: a persistent pre-occupation with an often unreasonable act.

Physical dependence-refers to a state resulting from chronic use of a drug that has produced tolerance and where negative physical symptom of withdrawal result from abrupt discontinuation or dosage reduction. Physical dependence can develop from low-dose therapeutic use of certain medications as well as misuse of recreational drugs such as alcohol. The higher the dose used typically the worse the physical dependence and thus the worse the withdrawal syndrome. Withdrawal syndromes can last days, weeks or months or occasionally longer and will vary according to the dose, the type of drug used and the individual person.

Psychoactive: mind or mood altering.

Psychotherapy: the psychological treatment of mental, emotional, and nervous   disorders.

Recidivism: a tendency to relapse into a previous condition or mode

Wierneke's Disease-Wernicke-Korsakoff syndrome- is commonly known as "Wet Brain". This is a brain disorder involving loss of specific brain functions caused by a thiamine deficiency as a result of alcoholism. It may also include symptoms caused by alcohol withdrawal. The cause is generally attributed to malnutrition, especially lack of vitamin B1 (thiamine), which commonly accompanies habitual alcohol use or alcoholism. Heavy alcohol use interferes with the metabolism of thiamine, so even in the unusual cases where alcoholics are eating a balanced diet while drinking heavily, the metabolic problem persists because most of the thiamine is not absorbed.

Given recent scientific knowledge about the biological and neurological causes of addiction, RWJF considers addiction to be a chronic health condition. As such, it should be treated like other chronic conditions with proven and accessible prevention and treatment methods. Yet, the needs of those who may become or are addicted go unmet when it comes to treatment and prevention.

What We've Supported

For more than two decades, the Foundation has sought to improve health by reducing the harmful effects of substance-use disorders and addictions. Early work centered on addiction prevention and education efforts, with special emphasis on underage drinking and drug use.

Over the years, our work in prevention and education has taught us that improving the quality of addiction treatment is essential to addressing the harms caused by addiction and other substance use. Therefore, the Foundation has focused more recently on improving treatment for alcohol and drug addictions.

We've supported work in three major areas:

Discouraging underage alcohol use and increasing the understanding of its harmful effects.

For example, we support *Reducing Underage Drinking Through Coalitions*, an effort to create coalitions at the state level that promote policies that limit underage access to alcohol.

Mobilizing communities and increasing public understanding about the harmful effects of drug use.

For example, we support *Partnership for a Drug-Free America*, a high-profile project that creates media-based public awareness campaigns about the harmful effects of misusing drugs.

Improving the quality and availability of treatment for those with substance-abuse disorders and addictions.

For example, we support Reclaiming Futures: Communities Helping Teens Overcome Drugs, Alcohol &

Crime, an innovative program aimed at making sure that when young people with addiction problems come in contact with the juvenile justice system, they get connected with appropriate treatment.

Key results and outcomes include:

Every dollar invested in substance abuse treatment yields $7 worth of economic benefits to society, according to a study partially funded by RWJF.

Screening and brief interventions for alcohol problems by emergency departments when patients present with injuries are effective in reducing health care costs, according to an RWJF-supported study. Recent research currently supports a number of projects to improve the quality of addiction treatment and will issue a call for proposals for our national program, *Advancing Recovery*, in June 2007, we do not envision making new investments in the specific area of quality of addiction treatment once these projects are complete. RWJF will honor and complete current grant commitments over the next several years to projects to improve the quality of addiction treatment services, and we can envision related grantmaking activities within the context of our Vulnerable Populations program area.

You may be hooked emotionally and psychologically. You may have a physical dependence, too. If you have a drug addiction, you have intense cravings for the drug. You want to use it again and again. When you stop taking it, you may have unpleasant physical reactions.

While not everyone who uses drugs becomes addicted, many people do. Drug addiction involves compulsively seeking to use a substance, regardless of the potentially negative social, psychological and physical consequences. Certain drugs are more likely to cause physical dependence than are others.

Breaking a drug addiction is difficult, but not impossible. Support from your doctor, family, friends and others who have a drug addiction, as well as inpatient or outpatient drug addiction treatment, may help you beat your drug dependence.

General signs and symptoms

Addiction to any drug may include these general characteristics:

- Feeling that you need the drug regularly and, in some cases, many times a day
- Making certain that you maintain a supply of the drug
- Failing repeatedly in your attempts to stop using the drug
- Doing things to obtain the drug that you normally wouldn't do, such as stealing
- Feeling that you need the drug to deal with your problems
- Driving or doing other activities that place you and others at risk of physical harm when you're under the influence of the drug

The particular signs and symptoms of drug use and dependence vary depending on the type of drug.

Cannabis compounds: Signs and symptom

Bibliography

Doweiko, Harold E. Concepts of Chemical Dependency. Brooks/Cole Publishing Company. Pacific Grove, Ca. 94002.,1990

Littrell, Jill. Understanding and treateing Alcoholism. **London, Lawrence Eulbaum, 1991.**

Milan, R. And K. Ketcham. Under the Influence. Seatle, Wa: Madrona Publishers, Inc., 1983

Royce, James E. Alcohol Problems @ Alcoholism: A comprehensive Survey. **The Free Press, A Division of McMillan,Inc., New York, New York, 1989**

Schuckit, M.A. Vulnerability factors for alcoholism, in Neuropsychopharmacology: The Fifth Generation of Progress, Chapter 98, pp. 1399-1411, Kenneth Davis (ed.), Lippincott Williams & Wilkins Co., Baltimore, 2002.

Schuckit, M.A., Smith, T.L. The relationships of a family history of alcohol dependence, a low level of response to alcohol and six domains of life functioning to the development of alcohol use disorders. J. Stud. Alcohol 61:827-835, 2000.

Schuckit, M.A., Edenberg, H.J., Kalmijn, J., et al. A genome-wide search for genes that relate to a low level of response to alcohol. Alcohol Clin Exp Res 25:323-329, 2001.

Schuckit, M.A., Mazzanti, C., Smith, T.L., et al. Selective genotyping for 6 receptors and the serotonin transporterγthe role of 5-HT2A , 5-HT2C , and GABA in the level of response to alcohol: a pilot study. Biol Psychiatry 45:647-651, 1999.